"How Goodly Are Thy Tents"

"How Goodly Are Thy Tents"

SUMMER CAMPS AS JEWISH SOCIALIZING EXPERIENCES

Amy L. Sales and Leonard Saxe

Brandeis University Press in association with The AVI CHAI Foundation

Published by University Press of New England

Hanover and London

Brandeis University Press in association with The AVI CHAI Foundation
Published by University Press of New England, 37 Lafayette St., Lebanon, NH 03766
© 2004 by Brandeis University Press

Printed in the United States of America

5 4 3 2

Library of Congress Cataloging-in-Publication Data
Sales, Amy L.
"How goodly are thy tents": summer camps as Jewish socializing
experiences / Amy L. Sales and Leonard Saxe.
    p.   cm. — (Brandeis series in American Jewish history, culture
and life)
Includes bibliographical references and index.
ISBN 1–58465–347–7 (pbk. : alk. paper)
1. Jewish camps—United States.   2. Jewish religious education—United
States.   3. Judaism—United States.   4. Camp counselors—Training
of—United States.   I. Saxe, Leonard.   II. Title.   III. Series.
BM 135.S25 2004
296.6′7—dc22   2003020815

Brandeis Series in American Jewish History, Culture, and Life

JONATHAN D. SARNA, Editor
SYLVIA BARACK FISHMAN, Associate Editor

Leon A. Jick, 1992
The Americanization of the Synagogue, 1820–1870

Sylvia Barack Fishman, editor, 1992
Follow My Footprints: Changing Images of Women in American Jewish Fiction

Gerald Tulchinsky, 1993
Taking Root: The Origins of the Canadian Jewish Community

Shalom Goldman, editor, 1993
Hebrew and the Bible in America: The First Two Centuries

Marshall Sklare, 1993
Observing America's Jews

Reena Sigman Friedman, 1994
These Are Our Children: Jewish Orphanages in the United States, 1880–1925

Alan Silverstein, 1994
Alternatives to Assimilation: The Response of Reform Judaism to American Culture, 1840–1930

Jack Wertheimer, editor, 1995
The American Synagogue: A Sanctuary Transformed

Sylvia Barack Fishman, 1995
A Breath of Life: Feminism in the American Jewish Community

Diane Matza, editor, 1996
Sephardic-American Voices: Two Hundred Years of a Literary Legacy

Joyce Antler, editor, 1997
Talking Back: Images of Jewish Women in American Popular Culture

Jack Wertheimer, 1997
A People Divided: Judaism in Contemporary America

Beth S. Wenger and Jeffrey Shandler, editors, 1998
Encounters with the "Holy Land": Place, Past and Future in American Jewish Culture

David Kaufman, 1998
Shul with a Pool: The "Synagogue-Center" in American Jewish History

Roberta Rosenberg Farber and Chaim I. Waxman, editors, 1999
Jews in America: A Contemporary Reader

Murray Friedman and Albert D. Chernin, editors, 1999
A Second Exodus: The American Movement to Free Soviet Jews

Stephen J. Whitfield, 1999
In Search of American Jewish Culture

Naomi W. Cohen, 1999
Jacob H. Schiff: A Study in American Jewish Leadership

Barbara Kessel, 2000
Suddenly Jewish: Jews Raised as Gentiles

Jonathan N. Barron and Eric Murphy Selinger, editors, 2000
Jewish American Poetry: Poems, Commentary, and Reflections

Steven T. Rosenthal, 2001
Irreconcilable Differences: The Waning of the American Jewish Love Affair with Israel

Pamela S. Nadell and Jonathan D. Sarna, editors, 2001
Women and American Judaism: Historical Perspectives

Annelise Orleck, with photographs by Elizabeth Cooke, 2001
The Soviet Jewish Americans

Ilana Abramovitch and Seán Galvin, editors, 2001
Jews of Brooklyn

Ranen Omer-Sherman, 2002
Diaspora and Zionism in American Jewish Literature: Lazarus, Syrkin, Reznikoff, and Roth

Ori Z. Soltes, 2003
Fixing the World: Jewish American Painters in the Twentieth Century

David Zurawik, 2003
The Jews of Prime Time

Ava F. Kahn and Marc Dollinger, editors, 2003
California Jews

Naomi W. Cohen, 2003
The Americanization of Zionism, 1897–1948

Gary P. Zola, editor, 2003
The Dynamics of American Jewish History: Jacob Rader Marcus's Essays on American Jewry

Judah M. Cohen, 2003
Through the Sands of Time: A History of the Jewish Community of St. Thomas, U.S. Virgin Islands

Seth Farber, 2003
An American Orthodox Dreamer: Rabbi Joseph B. Soloveitchik and Boston's Maimonides School

Amy L. Sales and Leonard Saxe, 2003
"How Goodly Are Thy Tents": Summer Camps as Jewish Socializing Experiences

To Daniel Saxe, an extraordinary camper,
and Leila Sales, counselor par excellence.

CONTENTS

FIGURES AND TABLES

ACKNOWLEDGMENTS

In August 2000, the American Jewish community was electrified by the announcement that Senator Joseph Lieberman, an observant Jew, had been selected by Democrats as their nominee for Vice President of the United States. For many Jews, the nomination signaled the breach of one of the few remaining barriers to their full acceptance. Senator Lieberman's Jewish observance was especially meaningful. By keeping kosher, observing the Sabbath, and speaking openly about his religious beliefs and God, he had declared to the world that being a practicing Jew was not incompatible with holding high public office. American Jews have achieved great professional and financial success, but this success has seemingly come through assimilation and the loss of distinctiveness. Senator Lieberman's unapologetic, "upfront" Judaism was symbolic of how Jews could be fully Jewish and still be successfully American.

We heard news of the nomination while en route to a site visit of a Jewish camp in the Northeast. Our summer had been spent traveling from one end of the country to the other in order to visit and study a variety of residential summer camps. The camps we studied were established primarily to provide a healthy summer environment for children. But we discovered that, as Jewish camps, they also provided settings with great power to socialize young campers and staff members. This book is about these camps and how they work their "magic" as socializing institutions.

Many of the issues we studied are not that different than issues attendant to the American Jewish community's reactions to Senator Lieberman's emergence as a national political figure. They concern the possibility of creating a generation of Jews who care deeply about their Judaism yet also hold a world outlook and function successfully as American citizens. And they concern the challenge of transmitting Jewish religion, culture, and pride to a younger generation that has increasingly fewer Jewish role models and influences. The questions that drove this study, however, are not solely parochial. They also relate to America's enduring social question of how simultaneously to be a "melting pot," to sustain religious and cultural diversity, and to build a society free of discrimination.

Motivated by these questions, we immersed ourselves in the study of Jewish summer camping. Armed with notepads, laptops, questionnaires, bug spray, and flashlights, we left the confines of our academic offices and headed out to the countryside to uncover the magic of camp. Our research quickly took on a structure and tone mirroring that of our subject matter. Camps are intentional communities dedicated to fun and committed to development and learning. So, too, was our work a communal effort, strengthened by the participation and support of many people. And it was a learning enterprise. Our "community" helped bring enormous amounts of data to bear on the topic and it forced us to keep an open mind with regard to the meaning of these data. The project was designed and carried out as a social scientific study, but, like camp, it also proved to be unmitigated fun.

The AVI CHAI Foundation had approached us the previous year with the idea of a study of Jewish summer camping. The foundation, whose mission is to promote Jewish education, had already invested a great deal in Jewish day schools. It was now considering other arenas in which it might support the growth and development of Jewish education. Camp was a relatively unknown but intriguing candidate. In supporting the research, the foundation insisted on useful, applicable findings. "If you come back with wonderful stories about your summer at camp but no recommendations of things we can do," they warned us, "you have not completed the task." They also insisted on pushing the boundaries of "Jewish camp" to include not only camps supported by various denominations and those with a specific educational mission, but also Jewish-owned camps that provide Jewish environments to large numbers of Jewish children during the summer. With both criticality and enthusiasm, they delved into our findings and pushed us toward ever greater clarity in our analysis. They were perhaps the first to see how serious fun can be and their generous and unending support allowed us to bring our research interests to fruition. Yossi Prager, Executive Director, Joel Einleger, Project Officer, and Arthur Fried, Chairman, managed simultaneously to motivate, critique, support, and inspire our work. We owe substantial gratitude to them and to the extraordinary members of the AVI CHAI board. Their imprint can be seen throughout the pages that follow.

We are also grateful to the foundation for their activist response to the results of our research. They studied and published our recommendations, hosted a conference in the fall of 2002 to bring the information and ideas to a broad audience of camp leaders and philanthropists, and quickly funded several initiatives that began to affect the field of Jewish summer camping even while we were still writing this book. Too often, research results are simply read and filed away. The AVI CHAI Foundation's activism has made our study a true bit of applied social science.

The camping study began at a time when the Foundation for Jewish Camping (FJC) had already been laboring in the field for several years. Our work very much benefited from the FJC's accomplishments. Rabbi Ramie Arian, Executive Director of FJC, gifted us with his database of Jewish summer camps and consulted to us throughout the project. One of our best readers, he aided with the accuracy of many details in our reports. Other colleagues also gave generously of their time. Charles Kadushin, Billy Mencow, Joseph Reimer and Jonathan Sarna read and commented on the manuscript. Ariella Feldman and Rabbi Allan Smith spent hours educating us about the field. Our own work has benefited greatly from their experience, wisdom, and honest feedback.

To preserve the anonymity of the camps we studied, we do not mention them by name. Nonetheless, our deepest thanks are also due to the directors who opened up their camps to us, welcomed us warmly, and, with complete frankness, shared with us the ups and downs of camp life. They housed us in guest houses and infirmaries, fed us in the dining hall, introduced us to staff, arranged meetings with counselors, and spent hours showing us around camp and telling us about their work and their vision.

As academics who study social phenomena like camps, we tend to respect the people who work on the front lines of the institutions we study. As our understanding of the complexity of the camping enterprise grew, so too did our respect, admiration, and affection for these leaders.

In the pages that follow, you will often see the words "we" or "our" in the discussion of camp site visits, observations, analyses, and interpretations of the data. The "we" is actually a research team based at Brandeis University's Maurice and Marilyn Cohen Center for Modern Jewish Studies. The team worked on every aspect of the project from design to interpretation. The wealth of data and ideas herein represent the collective contributions of our valued colleagues Fern Chertok, Simon Klarfeld, Laurie Mindlin, Mark Rosen, Larry Sternberg, and Diane Tickton Schuster. All of us were assisted ably in the field by student research assistants who smoothed our interactions with counselors (their peers), took copious notes, and offered unique insights into the meaning of the results. Our sincerest thanks go to Andrea Fram, Yuri Hronsky, Tali Hyman, Elliot Kaplowitz, Benjamin Phillips, Nicole Wilson, and Miranda Winer. A debt of thanks is also due to Daniel Victor and Joseph Fishman who spend hundreds of hours gathering data for the national census of Jewish camps. Matthew Boxer deserves special thanks for his help with database management and analysis. The energy, intelligence, and fun of this project are the product of this remarkably talented research team.

We also want to acknowledge our academic home and some of the key people who make our work possible. Gloria Tessler and Christie Cohen of our staff handle the administration of our projects and free us to think and write about the Jewish community. At the university, President Jehuda Reinharz has created an environment where serious scholarship is supported and where we can be unabashed in our interest in doing research that has practical value. The Cohen Center is particularly fortunate to have a dedicated Board of Advisors chaired by Robert Rifkind.

Special thanks go to our respective life partners, Michael Sales and Marion Gardner-Saxe. In their own ways, they provide the love and support that make it possible for us to do our work. Both Michael and Marion are busy professionals in their own right, but never too busy to listen to us talk about our work and to influence how we think about it. Each of us is also blessed to have a wonderful child, Leila Sales and Daniel Saxe. This book is dedicated to them. They have taught us more lessons than we can enumerate about life, about love, about growing up as Jewish children in America. They were both the subjects of this work and our best native informants and critics.

Today the air is frigid; the evergreens are outlined in white; and the city sounds are muffled by snow. But the sensations of summer camp float through our memories—the warmth of sunshine and friendship; the sounds of laughter, singing, and prayer; the smell of pine trees and sun lotion; and the taste of bug juice. Camp is a magical place and, in our role as social scientists, we have tried to deconstruct and explain this magic. To the extent we have succeeded, we hope that our research will benefit summer camps that strive to become pre-eminent educational and socializing institutions. Our message, we hope, will interest both those specifically concerned with the future of the Jewish community and those who are more generally concerned with how we socialize children in America. To the extent we have failed to capture some part of the magic, we hope that others will join us in trying to understand and nurture what summer camps have to offer. Camp deserves such attention because it appears to have nearly unlimited potential to produce joyous and memorable learning. It certainly produced such learning for us.

January 2003
A.S. and L.S.

1

Introduction

In the summer of 1954, two groups of young boys came to Robbers' Cave State Park in southeastern Oklahoma for three weeks of outdoor living, communal experiences, athletics, and fun. Robbers' Cave was the site for a summer camp that was neither an educational, nor a religious, nor a money-making enterprise. No ordinary camp, it was created by two social psychologists, Muzafer and Carolyn Sherif, in order to test hypotheses about how groups form and how intergroup conflict is created and extinguished. The boys who participated in the camp were subjects in what has become a classic study in social psychology (Sherif et al. 1961; Sherif and Sherif 1953). In addition to elucidating the nature of groups and intergroup relations, the findings from that study demonstrate the power of summer camps to socialize children and to mold their behavior and attitudes.

The two groups of campers arrived at Robbers' Cave in separate buses and, for the first week of camp, were kept isolated from and unaware of each other. In this insular environment, the boys developed intense bonds with one another and strong identification with their group. Each group spontaneously took on a name for itself, the Rattlers and the Eagles. Each group developed distinctive customs, norms, jargon, special jokes, secrets, unique ways of performing tasks, and preferred places. Leadership and roles, accompanied by appropriate nicknames, emerged in each group. Within a few days, each group had also developed a clear social organization.

After the first week, the Rattlers and the Eagles were brought together. So great was the boys' attachment to their own groups that a tournament between the two groups quickly devolved from good sportsmanship into hostility. The hostility, fueled by frustrating experiences engineered by the staff, led to animosity, name calling, physical encounters, food fights, and raids (with green apples the ammunition of choice). Asked to name whom they liked at camp, the boys limited themselves to members of their own group. Asked to estimate performance in contests, the boys routinely magnified the accomplishments of their own team and deprecated those of the opposing team.

During the third week of camp, the Sherifs tested ways to reduce conflict, overcome divisions, and build a peaceable camp community. Several attempts were made to bring the groups into contact and thereby change their behaviors and attitudes toward each other. Resolution was found only in the cumulative effect of activities that required the two groups to cooperate with each other in order to achieve a superordinate goal (i.e., a goal that was desired by both groups but could be achieved by neither alone). Everyone, whether Eagle or Rattler, needed to search in order to find the breakdown in the camp's water supply. The two teams needed to pool their money in order to rent a film that both wanted to see. En route to a distant lake, the truck that was to go for food stalled. To get the truck moving, all of the boys needed to pull together.

In the final act of that dramatic summer, the campers requested to go home together on the same bus rather than returning, as they had come, on separate buses. On the way home, the bus stopped for refreshments. The group that had won prize money in competitions at camp decided to spend its winnings on everyone—Rattlers and Eagles alike. The malted milks drunk that day signaled the lessons that had been learned at camp.

As social psychologists, we often use the Robbers' Cave experiment to exemplify the power of situations to shape individual behavior. In this study, camp is the background against which we learn about issues of group formation and conflict resolution. When we shift our focus, however, and move camp to the foreground, we see that it is a special environment in which young people can learn about themselves and experiment with a range of new behaviors. The features that made camp the ideal setting for the Sherifs' study are also those that make camp a highly effective socializing agent and a potential transmitter of religious and ethnic identity.

Why should camp be such an important setting for socialization? First, camp is an intense, enclosed setting. In the Robbers' Cave study, the camp setting removed the boys from their everyday environment and minimized the influences that typically loom large in a child's life (parents, classmates, media). The researchers were able to control the environment—how meals were served, which activities took place, when a truck would break down—in order to achieve desired effects. The campers, though, perceived the environment as natural and had no awareness of the study or the staff's manipulations. In social psychological terms, camp has both high experimental and high mundane realism (Aronson and Carlsmith 1968). Camp activities are absorbing; they hold children's attention. Despite the influence of adults, camp is experienced as a spontaneous event. It is also experienced as intensely real. Emotions at camp are passionate and the camp setting tends to amplify their expression, whether they be laughter, cheering, sadness, or anger.

Camp, by its nature, is also a laboratory in group life. As seen in the Robbers' Cave study, groups form virtually overnight at camp and intense relationships among campers grow. These relationships, the core of the camp experience, attract children to camp and form the essence of their camp memories. They also provide a framework for profound social learning.

Moreover, because summer camp lasts for several weeks, it provides the luxury of extended time with participants. Unlike scouts, after school clubs, or youth groups, camp offers continuous interaction among campers and between campers and staff. In the Robbers' Cave study, time allowed for the cumulative effect of cooperative intergroup activities. There was enough time for the campers to deal with a series of situations, all designed to pursue the same learning objective. The final lesson of the peaceable community could not have been learned in less time. Camp emphasizes learning through doing. At Robbers' Cave, there were no lectures or classes on intergroup cooperation. Rather, the profound learning of the summer came through living out the camp experience. The summer of

1954 was undoubtedly an unparalleled summer of experiential education for the boys involved. It most certainly left its mark on our notions of group dynamics and social learning.

The Robbers' Cave experiment did not directly inspire our own study of Jewish summer camps, but it attuned us to features of the environment that lend camp extraordinary power as a socializing agent. Our study of residential camps, carried out in the summers of 2000 and 2001, did not use camp as the setting for social experimentation. We neither manipulated the camp environment nor used campers as subjects. Rather, we observed camps *in vivo,* surveyed staff, and gathered systematic information about the range of Jewish camp experiences available. Like Sherif and Sherif, we recognized that camp is a special world, one with the potential to deeply affect the campers who inhabit it. Our goal was to understand how camps function to educate and socialize children. We were especially interested in the application of camp to the particular socialization tasks of the Jewish community.

SOCIALIZATION

Socialization is the process by which each of us acquires the knowledge, skills, and values needed to participate as effective members of a group. By its very nature, the process is concerned with people as social beings. It teaches us how to establish and maintain relationships with others and how to regulate our behavior in accordance with the group's codes and standards (Brim and Wheeler 1966; Craig 2000; Goslin 1969). Socialization is also implicated in identify formation. As we are socialized into a school, profession, or society, we not only take on the behaviors and attitudes appropriate for that group, but also come to see ourselves as members of the group. Membership in the group becomes a part of our social identity. Socialization is thus the key mechanism by which groups sustain themselves as it binds new members to the group and transmits the group's values and knowledge from one generation to the next.

Socialization is one of two core social development processes. The other is individuation, the process of defining ourselves as unique and distinct from others in the group. Individuation leads to personal identity, an aggregate of personal qualities, characteristics, and abilities that define each of us as an individual. The capacity to form satisfying relationships with others and with the group depends on both socialization and individuation. It requires a self-image that has integrated both social and personal identities (Brown 1986; Craig 2000).

Just as every child is socialized as a member of his or her society, so too, must Jewish children be socialized as members of the Jewish people. Nothing less is at stake than Jewish strength and survival. Jewish socialization involves acquiring the knowledge, skills, and attitudes that enable one to be an active member of the Jewish community. It is concerned with forming both a social and a personal identity as a Jew. These two processes are intertwined: As a child learns about the community and what it takes to be a member, the child also gains greater clarity about who he or she is and how he or she personally fits in. Given the nature of Jewish identity, this task touches on questions related not only to religion, but also to ancestry, nationality, ethnicity, and values. Moreover, this task is not completed within a single period of development but rather extends across the life span, from infancy through adulthood (Horowitz 2000).

Socialization and Community

A community's unity, strength, and continuation depend on its capacity to socialize new members—to build commitment to the group and to transmit its knowledge and values to each succeeding generation. Socialization is thus critical to the Jewish enterprise, which is based in community. At the core of Judaism's wisdom is Rabbi Hillel's injunction not to separate oneself from the community (*Pirkei Avot*, 2.6). At the core of Jewish practice are public Torah readings, rituals, and prayers that require a *minyan*, ten members of the community who comprise the necessary quorum for performing these acts. At the core of its ideology is the notion of a Covenant between God and the Jewish people. Centered thus on the idea of peoplehood, Judaism depends on the communal entity for its existence and continuation (Eisen 1990; Lipset and Rabb 1995).

It has long been recognized that Jewish life in America cannot and would not exist without community-mindedness and communal organization (Kaplan 1934). Despite the power of individualism in American society, Jews continue to create vital Jewish life because it offers them meaning and community—two precious commodities not easily found elsewhere (Bellah et al. 1986; Eisen 1992). The community, in turn, sustains the Jewish life forms that emerge from this desire to identify with something greater than the self. In this way, community is both the source and the product of Jewish life. Diminishment of community means a decline in Jewish life, and vice versa.

Evidence from socio-demographic studies conducted in recent years, in fact, indicates a weakening of community ties in the Jewish population (Cohen, Fein, and Israel 2000; Goldstein and Goldstein 1995). Jewish social indices are all highly interrelated: Inmarriage, affiliation, philanthropic giving, connection to Israel, and social networks are consistently found to co-vary. They increase together, creating at times an upward spiral effect, but they also decline in unison. The greatest weakening, perhaps, is in American Jews' diachronic view of their link to Jewish history and synchronic view of their link to the Jewish people. As captured by Cohen and Eisen (2000) in *The Jew Within*, contemporary American Jews appear more likely to find meaning in the personal realm and immediate institutions (e.g., synagogues and Jewish community centers) than in the public sphere or in the grand sense of Jewish history and peoplehood.

Similar declines, in both the public and private spheres, are found in American society in general. Robert Putnam (2000) documents declines in church attendance, voting, political interest, campaign activities, association membership, social trust, club meetings, neighboring, visiting with friends, and, what he calls "schmoozing" (e.g., card playing or entertaining at home). The causes of this loss of "social capital" are complex. A small part of the loss is attributable to factors such as economic distress, the pressures associated with two-career families, and suburbanization and sprawl. A somewhat larger percentage is attributable to the isolating effects of television and other media, as every hour spent watching television is time lost to social activities. According to Putnam, however, the declines in the public realm are a generational phenomenon, largely accounted for by the succession of the "Greatest Generation" by the "Baby Boomers" and their children. With regard to American civic involvement, American Jews are likely influenced by these factors in the same way as the general population. What we do not know, however, is whether these same factors are also causing declines in Jews' engagement in Judaism and in Jewish social and political activities.

Nonetheless, the organized Jewish community is responding to the challenge of reduced engagement. Across the contemporary Jewish landscape, numerous efforts are underway to put community involvement at center stage. Local Jewish community centers are working toward "meaningful community" (Cohen, Fein, and Israel 2000). SYNAGOGUE 2000, an interdenominational renewal effort, is attempting to transform synagogues into "sacred communities" (Hoffman 2002; Hoffman and Wolfson 1999). The religious movements are promoting the idea of "caring communities."

Rhetoric about "community" is intentional. It is an attempt to reframe Jewish organizations as communities and to turn customers into members. In recent years, Jews increasingly have joined Jewish community centers, synagogues, and other organizations as consumers. They are there to purchase services: access to a health club, religious education for children, seats in the sanctuary for High Holiday services. In synagogues, one result is what Wolfson (nd) calls "the frequent flyer synagogue" or Hoffman (1980, 2002) refers to as the "synagogue of limited liability." Such synagogues breed little identification with or commitment to the congregation. Once a family no longer requires the particular service (e.g., their children's education is completed), it simply drops out. Membership in the community has little meaning for them and plays a negligible role in their social identities. If ties are weak in the personal or local realm, they will be even weaker in the public or global realm. The desired outcome of attempts to build community, therefore, are not only to deepen the sense of belonging to a particular organization and local community, but also to fashion bonds to the Jewish people writ large (Cohen, Fein, and Israel 2000).

If community is at the heart of the Jewish enterprise and if the future of Judaism and Jewish life reside in the capacity to build strong communities, then socialization becomes the core task of the collective. Through socialization, people come to identify with the group and to feel a part of it. They internalize its values, and they learn its norms and behaviors. The community will flourish only to the extent that it succeeds in socializing young members into the fold.

SOCIALIZING AGENTS

There is considerable evidence that parents, as the primary caregivers, play a special and central role in the socialization of their children. Nonetheless, it is also now widely recognized that the socialization process involves many people, not just parents, and many institutions, not just families (Bugental and Goodnow 1997; Grusec and Kuczynski 1997; Harris 1995). In recent decades, psychologists and sociologists have expanded their research on socialization to include a wide range of environments from immediate settings (e.g., neighborhood) to broad systems that may affect children only indirectly (e.g., parents' workplace; see Bronfenbrenner 1979; Garbarino, Kostelny and Barry 1997). This expansion of the study of socialization parallels developments in the American Jewish community that have lessened reliance on the family for Jewish socialization.

Modernity, Americanization, suburbanization, assimilation, and social acceptance are concepts that encapsulate the story of American Jewry in the twentieth century. Each has led to a loss of the traditional socializing agents that had previously transmitted Jewish understanding in an "organic" way from one generation to the next. By the latter part of the century, children in the mainstream Jewish community could no longer learn about being Jewish simply by osmosis—from living in a homogeneous Jewish neighborhood, from being raised in a knowledgeable family committed to Jewish life, from being surrounded by a network of Jewish friends and extended family. To compensate for this loss, the Jewish community created an extensive system of schools and informal education programs. These institutions grew into a billion-dollar enterprise that employed tens of thousands of educators and staff (Commission on Jewish Education in North America 1991; Wertheimer 1999). Parents have largely accepted the community's help in the socialization of their children, relying on synagogues, day schools, and camps as the family's partners (or proxies) in this enterprise. It is thus often the case that children acquire Jewish skills that their parents lack, and indeed, may not even want for themselves (Prell 2000).

School
By most accountings, at least half of Jewish children in the United States receive some type of formal Jewish education (Kosmin et al. 1991). Most of these, perhaps 60 percent, attend one of nearly two thousand supplementary religious schools (Aron 1995; Commission on Jewish Education in North America 1991; Wertheimer 1999). These schools, generally housed in synagogues, meet one to three times per week (on weekends and week-

days after school). According to research conducted in the 1990s, the effect of extensive Jewish education can be seen in every area of an individual's public and private Jewish life. The more intense their Jewish education, the more likely people are to attend worship services regularly, to be religiously observant, to develop Jewish social networks, to feel close to Israel, and to identify strongly as Jews (S. M. Cohen 1995; Schiff and Schneider 1994).

Despite this evidence, the power of the supplementary school to transform Jewish youth into active participants in Jewish life and community is questionable. Our own prior research (Kadushin, Kelner, and Saxe 2000) makes clear that supplementary education is a troubled enterprise. Adolescents dislike religious school more than they do their secular school and they take it less seriously. Rabbi Eric Yoffie, president of the Reform movement's Union of American Hebrew Congregations, admits that many parents look upon religious school as the ". . . castor oil of Jewish life, a burden passed from parent to child with the following admonition: 'I hated it, you'll hate it, and after your *bar mitzvah,* you can quit'" (Yoffie 2001).

Moreover, children whose education comes primarily from the synagogue religious school have too few hours a week in a Jewish environment to be well socialized into the Jewish community. Even the most demanding programs provide insufficient hours to transmit the complex set of norms, values, and skills required for participation in Jewish life (Zeldin 1989).

One response has been serious examination of current educational programs, experimentation with new forms, and a revamping of old programs (e.g., Holtz 1993; Taskforce on Congregational and Communal Jewish Education 2000). The impulse toward innovation has led to the establishment of programs of Jewish family education (Bank and Wolfson 1998; Sales, Koren, and Shevitz 2000), the Reform movement's Experiment in Congregational Education (Aron 1995; 2000), and other such attempts at educational reform and improvement.

A second response has been increased investment in Jewish day schools. It is estimated that the Jewish day school population tripled between the mid-1960s and the end of the 1990s (cf. Schick 2000). This surge in enrollment was, in part, the result of the establishment of new types of day schools, including community day schools and day schools affiliated with the Reform movement. It was, in part, fostered by a crisis in public-school education, the relatively lower tuition fees of day schools versus other private schools, and the attitude of Baby Boomer parents who wanted to give their children more intensive and enjoyable Jewish schooling than they themselves had had. It was also fueled by increases in the Orthodox population and outreach to the children of new immigrants (Wertheimer 1999). Indeed, Wertheimer concludes that the "herculean labors to establish and maintain day schools is one of the epic—and underappreciated—sagas of late twentieth-century American Jewry" (p. 57).

Camp, Israel, and Youth Group

Another response to the shortcomings of the supplementary religious schools has been interest in informal Jewish education. Informal Jewish education is based on the premise that meaningful learning results from direct, personal connection to the subject matter (Dewey 1964). It is characterized by participants' active involvement in the educational process and by their positive motivation. Unlike school, informal education is voluntary (Chazan 1991). This fundamental difference permeates every aspect of the experience, from the participant's initial attitude to the program's final impact. The difference between formal and informal education resides primarily in pedagogical approach and not in setting. That is, it is possible to have formal education by the lake and informal education in a classroom. Nonetheless, in the Jewish world, informal education is generally associated with youth groups, summer camps, and Israel experiences.

Zeldin (1989) describes formal education's "hidden curriculum," which conveys its lessons through the environment and the social group, and not through textbooks or frontal teaching. The outcomes of this hidden curriculum are the norms, values, and ideas that students learn even though teachers do not teach them directly. In Jewish education, these outcomes might include the sense that Judaism is joyous or the understanding that prayer is a creative experience. In informal Jewish education, the hidden curriculum becomes the overt curriculum. It is this reversal in approach that characterizes Jewish camping experiences.

Informal Jewish education is on the ascendancy. Schools of Jewish communal services have helped legitimate experiential education by training professionals in its theory and practice. Since the mid-1970s, the Coalition for the Advancement of Jewish Education (CAJE) has worked to bridge the gap between educators working in formal educational settings and those working in informal settings.[1] Recent years have seen increasing professionalization and a clearer sense of definition in the field of informal Jewish education. There is now an international association of informal Jewish education organizations that holds an annual conference (North American Alliance, founded in 1997) and an academic institution devoted to research and professional training (Institute for Informal Jewish Education, Brandeis University, founded in 1998).

The crown jewel of informal Jewish education has been the Israel experience, which was heralded in the 1990s as the antidote to teenagers' Jewish malaise. A number of Israel education initiatives (led, notably, by Israel Experience Inc. and, later, by birthright israel) were designed to bring more young American Jews to Israel.[2] Youth movements and private trip purveyors offered a panoply of travel experiences ranging from arts programs to sports adventures in Israel. Extensive evaluation research was undertaken to document the impact of the trips on participants (e.g., Chazan 1997; E. H. Cohen 1994, 1995; Goldberg, Heilman, and Kirshenblatt-Gimblett 2002; Mittelberg 1999, Saxe et al. 2002).[3] The community poured its resources and its hopes into the Israel experience.

Research consistently demonstrates that educational trips to Israel have a measurable impact on participants, whether they are teens or young adults. Participants express high levels of satisfaction with the trip and report thinking a great deal about Israel and their friends from the trip, even months afterwards. Compared to those who apply but do not go on the birthright israel program, participants show substantial change in their attitudes toward and identification with Israel and the Jewish people (Saxe et al. 2002). Perhaps the most interesting outcome is that these programs create an extraordinary sense of community and group identification. Asked what aspect of the trip had the greatest personal impact, one participant on a teen trip wrote: "I have to say that traveling with my group most affected me. Living with people for a straight month, having *Shabbat* services with them, not showering for four days with them, singing with them, and going to the [Western] Wall with them brought me closer to these people than I have ever been to anyone and taught me a lot about myself" (Sales 1999). These few words capture the essence of informal Jewish education.

Limitations of Jewish Socializing Agents

Perhaps not surprisingly, the Jewish community has repeatedly sought a so-called "magic bullet," a single defining way to transform a child into a lifelong adherent to Judaism (cf. Abramowitz 1998). However, research suggests that despite the immediate emotional benefits of a trip to Israel or a summer at camp, no single intervention changes the trajectory of a child's Jewish life. Rather, adult outcomes appear to be linked to an accumulation of positive Jewish experiences. In her study of adult Jewish identity, Horowitz (2000) found that the particular type of experience (whether youth group, camp, Israel trip, and/or college activities) was not as important as the fact that it was voluntary rather than required. Importantly, she found no group in her complex sample of American Jews for whom camp or Israel was a magic bullet of Jewishness. Horowitz concludes that the impact of a summer in Israel or at a dynamic Jewish camp depends upon the individual's history and a combination of personal factors and experiences. Her conclusions are cautionary: The outcomes of Jewish socialization efforts are difficult to predict, and they certainly are not guaranteed.

Moreover, no single socializing agent can build a child's Jewish identity, teach Jewish skills, convey the fullness of Jewish learning, build a commitment to Jewish values, and instill an emotional connection to Judaism and the Jewish people. Even the Israel experience is not a panacea. Although it succeeds in building a connection to Israel, its effect on *Shabbat* observance and other religious practices is much less obvious. After reviewing the accumulated research on the impact of the Israel experience, Chazan (1997) concludes that "the Israel Experience is not a substitute for intensive synagogue life, high quality Jewish schooling, a rich Jewish family life or quality informal education, but rather is a valuable partner and complement to these institutions" (p. 4).

Given the complexity of Jewish socialization, Jewish youth need a variety of socializing agents. In an ideal world, socialization tasks could be neatly divided among institutions, with parents and the home environment transmitting tradition and building Jewish identity, Jewish schools teaching religious skills, Jewish history, and culture, and youth groups and summer camps providing Jewish role models and social contacts (Keysar et al. 2000). The ideal assumes that each of the institutions is prepared to fulfill its socializing role and that every child is exposed to these various influences. Regardless of the actual division of labor, socialization takes place through the aggregation of these influences, and no single institution can or should be expected to carry the sole responsibility.

Finally, there is growing acceptance of the idea that Jewish socialization is not simply an intellectual process but also involves behaviors and feelings. Formal education may succeed at imparting knowledge and teaching skills, but it may fail at instilling love, commitment, and clear identity. Feeling Jewish and doing Jewish things, Heilman (1992) argued, may be the prerequisite to becoming a stronger Jew. Herein lies the unique contribution of Jewish summer camps and other programs of informal Jewish education. With their focus on experiential activities, group techniques, and concern with individual growth, they support the creation of Jewish friendships and Jewish self-identification. They create for children positive associations with Judaism.

SOCIALIZATION PROCESSES

While sociologists study the agents of socialization, psychologists attempt to understand socialization processes, the mechanisms by which children learn to be members of the community. At the foundation of psychological theories of socialization are interpersonal interactions, for it is through relationships with others that the learner is turned into an effective member of the group.

Key to our study of socialization processes at summer camps are Kelman's (1961) ideas about social influence. Kelman is concerned with how one person influences another to adopt new behaviors, attitudes, and values. He distinguishes three levels of influence: compliance, identification, and internalization. Compliance is based on the desire to gain reward or avoid punishment. Behavior induced by compliance depends on the power of the influencer to mete out rewards and punishments, and it typically lasts only as long as these are operative. Identification is based on our desire to be like the other person. It impels us to take on behaviors or opinions in order to be in a satisfying relationship with the influencer.

Internalization of values or beliefs is the most permanent, most deeply rooted response to social influence. It is based on our desire to be right and depends on the extent to which we see the influencer as credible and trustworthy. Once a belief or value has been integrated, it takes on its own life and becomes highly resistant to change. Children are more likely to internalize societal values and behaviors, to make them their own, when less (rather than more) pressure is applied. The socialization challenge, then, is to promote socially sanctioned behavior "without killing the spirit of the child, without diminishing the child's natural curiosity, vitality, and excitement" (Grolnick, Deci, and Ryan 1997, p. 135). Camp, as we will see, meets this challenge.

Two additional sources of social learning are relevant to the summer camp experience. One source is direct experience. Research indicates that attitudes formed through direct experience are stronger than those formed through vicarious experience (see e.g., Fazio and Zanna 1981). This finding suggests that the attitudes toward Judaism that result from experiencing Jewish practices at camp will be held with more confidence and be more resistant to change than attitudes that might be formed through books or lectures at religious school.

The other source is imitation, which some argue is the most important source of social learning (Bandura 1977; Bandura and Walters 1963). According to social learning theory, a person begins to learn new behaviors by first observing models. The more models the learner sees engaging consistently in the same behavior, the more the learner will imitate those models (e.g., Fehrenbach, Miller, and Thelen 1979). As will be seen in later chapters, camps are replete with models, the most important of whom are counselors. In the best of circumstances, counselors can display consistent Jewish behaviors, day after day, thus creating the necessary condition for campers to imitate and learn these behaviors.

Social Learning at Camp

Camps are structured to be socializing agents. Every camp, regardless of religious orientation, sponsorship, or educational program, places great importance on social relations, friendship formation, and community building. The camp day abounds with opportunities for direct experience, imitation, and the kinds of relationships that encourage identification and internationalization of new values and behaviors.

Camper-staff relations. Much of the Jewish learning at camp occurs through the medium of the camper-counselor relationship. Compliance is certainly in evidence at camp. Staff do not hesitate to use competition and rewards to induce certain behaviors, including behaviors related to sacred activities, such as decorum at worship services, and those related to Jewish values, such as respect for others. More evident, however, is the role of staff as influencers whom the campers find attractive and trustworthy. Counselors influence their campers through role modeling and through encouraging them to "try on" new behaviors.

Camper-camper relations. The psychological literature documents how peers also socialize each other. For example, young children teach each other appropriate modes of conflict resolution, cooperative play, and self-disclosure. Adolescents help each other in the construction of new stable and cohesive identities, a key task of this stage of development (e.g., Kuczynski, Marshall, and Schell 1997). Peer socialization depends on the quality of the relationship. Relationships characterized by greater closeness, frequency of interaction, and positive emotional expression are more influential in the development of internalized values and behaviors than are less-close relationships (e.g., Haan 1985; Nelson and Aboud 1985). These findings suggest that camp can greatly amplify peer influences. Campers live, work, and play together intensively over several weeks. The setting and the culture of camp engender deep bonding and intimacy. In addition, camp is fun. There is great support and encouragement for campers, little criticality or evaluation, and no tests or grades. Camp is suffused with positive emotional expression. These are precisely the conditions that allow young people to influence each other's behavior, opinions, and values.

Staff as social learners. The great majority of staff at Jewish summer camps are between the ages of eighteen and twenty-five, a time of life referred to as emerging adulthood (cf. Arnett 2000). This period of life is a recent development in American society that has resulted from several trends: later marriage, postponement of first childbirth, and increases in the percentages of young people attending college and pursuing postgraduate education (Arnett 2000; Goldstein 1992; U.S. Bureau of the Census 1998). The overall result of these trends is that the late teens and early twenties have become a long and gradual bridge between adolescence and adulthood—a time of exploration and profound change. Indeed, when adults retrospectively consider the most important events in their lives, they most often name events that took place during this period (Arnett 2000). Emerging adults have left the dependency of childhood and adolescence but they have not as yet entered the "enduring responsibilities" of adulthood (Arnett 2000; Erikson 1968). It is a time when they can explore various options in love, work, and worldviews without the oversight of their parents and without the obligation to settle down and earn an adult living. For most people, exploration of life's possibilities is greater during these years than it will be at any other period of their life. And the decisions they make during this time will reverberate throughout their adulthood (Arnett 2000; Arnett, Ramos and Jensen 2001; Martin and Smyer 1990).

Relevant to the Jewish community is the fact that most identity exploration takes place in emerging adulthood rather than during adolescence. Identity development is not completed during high school but rather continues through the late teens and into the twenties. Research on religious beliefs supports this view and suggests that these years are also a time when people reexamine the beliefs learned in their families and form a personal set of beliefs based on their own independent reflections (Arnett 2000). Not surprisingly, experiences such as a trip to Israel or a summer at camp have been found to have a greater impact on college students than they do on high school students (Bardin 1992; Israel and Mittelberg 1998; Mittelberg 1999).

Camp, as our research will make clear, is an environment designed explicitly for trying out new behaviors and exploring questions of personal identity and values. Camp founders intended this environment to serve campers' developmental needs. However, they unintentionally created a near-perfect environment for the young adult counselors who, perhaps even more than the campers, are in the process of exploring options and setting the pathway for their future.

CAMPS AS JEWISH SOCIALIZING AGENTS

Socialization addresses the American Jewish community's concern with assimilation and the fading of Jewish life. It focuses not on pedagogy, text, and curricula, but on human relationships and their role in personal and social development. Given the socialization challenge—the need for multiple socializing agents and alternative educational environments, the importance of affective learning, and the value of immersion experiences—it is not surprising that the community has begun to look toward summer camping. If camping is not a magic bullet, then at least it is a key socializing agent worthy of resources and study. Heightened communal interest in camping as a force in Jewish education is evidenced in a host of community and philanthropic initiatives undertaken in the late 1990s and early 2000s. Many are coming to agree with Rabbi Ramie Arian (2002), director of the Foundation for Jewish Camping, who says that "Jewish camps are a precious but under-appreciated resource, a resource which the community should cherish and grow" (p. 3).

Commensurate with the heightened attention to Jewish summer camping are increases in participation. A greater percentage of the Jewish population attends Jewish camps today than was the case three or four decades ago (Cohen 1999, 2000; Tobin and Weinstein 2000). This generational change, it should be noted, parallels similar increases in teen Israel experiences and participation in youth groups. Two forces appear to be at work: The community is offering more, and more people are choosing to take advantage of the opportunities (Cohen 2000). Jewish camping may be reaching the tipping point (Gladwell 2000), the moment at which the idea and experience of a summer at a Jewish camp becomes "contagious" and spreads throughout the community.

Our study validates this increased interest in Jewish summer camping by documenting the ways in which camp can be an effective socializing agent. Camps create the type of environment and encourage the kinds of relationships that are most likely to lead to social learning. These elements are readily applied to the task of Jewish socialization. Camp envelops campers and staff in a Jewish environment for an extended period of time and it gives them a sweet taste of Judaism. Camp exposes campers and staff to Jewish leaders and role models who exhibit Jewish identity, *ruach* (spirit), and *menschlichkeit* (being a good person). Some camps also educate campers and staff, teaching them Jewish history and Torah. Our preference, however, is to move beyond the bifurcation of the Jewish camping world into those camps that are considered "educational camps" and those that are presumably non-educational. Rather, we believe that every Jewish camp ipso facto has the potential to socialize Jewish children and young adults into *k'lal Yisrael* (the Jewish people).

STUDY OF CAMPING

As behavioral scientists, even if not operating in the experimentalist tradition of Sherif and Sherif's Robbers' Cave research, we viewed the complex community of camp through a social scientific lens. Our approach was inherently interdisciplinary and our work encompassed approaches taken by psychologists, sociologists, and anthropologists. We used multiple methods to triangulate an understanding of how Jewish summer camps transmit culture and religious values to those who are part of their communities. These methods included a national census of Jewish residential camps, a participant-observation field study, organizational analyses of camps, and social psychological surveys of the attitudes and motivations of the young adults who work at camp. Conducted over a two-year period from 2000 to 2002, our study, like any research, is necessarily time-bound. It provides a snapshot of a moving stream that continues to flow and change.

Our analysis of Jewish camps as socializing institutions begins in chapter 2 with a bird's-eye view of the field of Jewish residential camps. Based on our national census of Jewish camps, it presents data on the range of experiences available and on the number of Jewish children and emerging adults who partake of these experiences. The next five chapters are an inside look at camps based on our survey and field research. Chapter 3, "Camp is Camp," explains the characteristics of residential camps that can make them powerful socializing environments for young people. Chapter 4, "Candy, Not Castor Oil," describes the varieties of formal and informal Jewish education found at camp. Chapter 5, "The Fresh Air of Judaism," presents observations on everyday and religious practices, Jewish space and symbolism, and other aspects of the physical environment that, in the aggregate, express the quality of Jewish life and spirit at camp. Chapter 6, "The Counselor as Teacher and Friend," presents data from the perspective of the professional staff—the directors, educators, and counselors who create the social environment necessary for Jewish socialization. Chapter 7, "Valleys and Peaks of Staff Development," focuses on the emerging adults at camp and analyzes the potential impact of a summer at a Jewish residential camp on their life choices. We conclude in chapter 8, "Building a Better Tent," with a consideration of the ways in which the field of Jewish summer camping might evolve in order to become a model of and inspiration for Jewish education and community.

2

The Landscape

A CENSUS OF JEWISH RESIDENTIAL CAMPS

From Moses' accounting of "all the congregations of Israel" as instructed by God after the exodus from Egypt (Num. 1:2) to the contemporary decennial National Jewish Population Survey (cf. Kosmin et al. 1991), the Jewish people have been concerned with questions of "how many?" Our study, too, began with the question of numbers: How many camps fall under the rubric of "Jewish camp"? How many campers do they serve? How many Jewish staff members do they employ? To answer these questions and establish the context of our research, we carried out a national census of mainstream Jewish residential camps. Using camp directories, informants, advertisements, and public records, we identified 191 camps that have a Jewish owner or sponsor, are largely populated by Jewish campers, and self-identify as a Jewish camp. All of these camps serve as socializing agents for their campers, teaching them how to function in groups and how to live in community. The census was designed to count "how many" and to document the features of these camps that enable them to serve as *Jewish* socializing agents, teaching their campers what it means to be a Jew and to be part of the Jewish community.

The results of the census show great diversity among Jewish overnight camps and little uniformity regarding their Jewish life and learning. Some are camps with formal Jewish sponsorship, where Judaism is an explicit element of camp life. Bunks have Hebrew names, daily prayers are recited, and *Shabbat* is a central part of the camp experience. Others are nonde-nominational or pluralistic private camps with Jewish owners and campers but few intentional Jewish activities. Bunks may have Native American names, no formal times are set aside for daily prayer, and *Shabbat* may be acknowledged only minimally. Still others operate somewhere between these two extremes.

SIZE AND SHAPE OF THE JEWISH CAMP WORLD

Several prior attempts have been made to estimate the size of the Jewish camp world and there has been some dispute as to actual numbers of children under the camp tent (cf. Bardin 1992; Mono 2001). The dispute rests, in part, on where the boundary of Jewish camping is drawn and, in part, on the number of identified camps providing information about their operations.

Our criteria for inclusion in the census were liberal. Our intent was not to limit the study to so-called educational camps, but rather to study the full array of Jewish camp environments in the United States where children spend their summers. Camps were thus included in the census if they met all three of the following conditions: (1) The camp has Jewish owners or is sponsored by a Jewish organization; (2) at least half of the campers are Jewish; and (3) the camp identifies itself as a Jewish camp.

Our search for Jewish camps began with a database assembled by the Foundation for Jewish Camping (1999). We then moved to camp directories in print and on the Internet, camp advertisements in the Jewish newspapers of major metropolitan areas, and information from friends and colleagues about camps popular with the Jewish families in their communities. Some of the camps were specifically designated as Jewish camps in the camp directories. In other instances, we looked for clues that a camp might be Jewish. For example, the clue for one camp was an indication of "kosher-style" food. For another, it was a listing of *bar mitzvah* celebrations in the camp's on-line newsletter. The clue for a third was a list with "bullets" in the shape of Jewish stars. This effort generated an initial list of over 200 camps. The director of each of these camps was sent a four-page survey requesting basic information about the camp, its population, its budget, and its Jewish programming. Extensive follow-up via mail, fax, e-mail, and telephone enabled us to obtain core data on every camp.

After eliminating camps that did not meet all three of our criteria, we arrived at a final list of 191 Jewish camps. The list is comprehensive with respect to camps whose practices fall in the range of liberal to traditional Judaism. It includes camps run by the religious and Zionist movements, community agencies, foundations, and private owners. It does not include the Hasidic and ultra-Orthodox camps, often run by rabbis or sectarian *yeshivot* (religious schools). Because these camps are, in essence, closed systems that serve a particular community, either we could not identify them or they were not interested in participating in the research. Perhaps only one in five of the yeshiva camps and none of the Hasidic Satmar camps are included. The latter serves an estimated summer population of between 6,000 and 12,000 campers.

In total, the 191 "mainstream" residential camps included in the census serve approximately 83,000 Jewish children during the summer. If the ultra-Orthodox camps were included, this number would likely rise to about 100,000. In addition, approximately 18,000 Jewish adults work at a Jewish overnight camp during the summer. The vast majority of these staff members are emerging adults between the ages of eighteen and twenty-four. The result is an annual flowering of Jewish youth communities, populated with tens of thousands of children, teens, and young adults, that for two months of the year create a form of Jewish communal life out in the countryside.

Types of Jewish Camps

Some in the Jewish community believe that camps with no educational content should be excluded from a census of Jewish camps or that the world should, at least, be divided into two categories: camps that provide study sessions or Jewish educational activities and those that do not. About 60 percent of the camps in our census have an explicit educational component and 40 percent do not. As we argue in succeeding chapters, however, education at camp takes place in myriad ways, both implicit and explicit, and the presence of formal Jewish study is not the sine qua non of Jewish camping.

Rather, camps are more usefully distinguished by their sponsorship. Using sponsorship/ownership as the criterion, we divided the world of Jewish residential camps into seven types (table 2.1). This typology cap-

Table 2.1. Types of Jewish Camps

Sponsorship/ownership	Number
Community	
Jewish federation/Jewish community center	35
Agency/organization	32
Movement	
Zionist	15
Denominational	18
Private	
Non-Orthodox for-profit	64
Foundation/independent nonprofit	15
Orthodox for-profit	12
Total	191

tures differences in organizational structure (i.e., camp governance and finances), ideology (i.e., independence from or connection to a movement), and the intentionality of the camp's Jewish character. Through our observational study, we learned that sponsorship influences every aspect of camp related to Jewish life and learning, from the camp's philosophy to its daily practices, activities, staffing, and clientele. One denominational movement camp, for example, estimates that 80 percent of its campers come from within the movement. At the other extreme, a Jewish federation camp reports that many of its campers are being raised in homes with little Jewish involvement. In the former case, the camp works consistently within the parameters of the movement. In the latter case, the camp is necessarily sensitive to the fact that for many of the participants, camp is "their only connection to something Jewish."

Community camps. The first Jewish camps were those run by local Jewish community agencies and organizations. The oldest of these were founded in 1902—Surprise Lake, a Jewish federation camp in New York, and Tamarack Camps, two camps sponsored by the Fresh Air Society in Michigan (Bice 2002). In these early years, camp was an affordable way for lower class children, often of immigrant families, to escape the congestion, heat, and disease of the city. Chaim Potok (1993), the author, recalled being sent to camp in the 1930s and 1940s to escape the summer polio epidemics. "I grew up in New York," he wrote, "where the fear of that illness was so overwhelming that my father, a deeply religious man brought to ruin by the Great Depression, would send me to non-kosher Jewish overnight camps sponsored by local community centers, the only free camps available to us. Breathe the fresh air, he would say. Have a good time. He did not say what I read on his face and in his eyes: I am sending you out of the city so you will be far away from this sickness that is crippling children" (p. 5). As Potok describes, the first Jewish camps were established literally to save the lives of Jewish children.

Jewish community centers, Jewish federations, and various religious, educational, and social welfare agencies built camps throughout the twentieth century. Such camps account for about one-third of the Jewish residential camps currently on the landscape. Although they have moved beyond the original purpose of the agency camps, these camps still maintain, on average, among the lowest tuitions of the Jewish camps and offer scholarships to a significant number of their campers (see table 2.7). About one-third of the camps in this category are sponsored by Orthodox organizations. Most of the others, however, are nondenominational, serving children of varied Jewish backgrounds and often reaching those with weak ties to organized Jewish life.

Zionist camps. By the 1930s, summer camp had become a mass phenomenon with widespread appeal throughout the Jewish community. It "engaged the collective imagination of the left and the right, the working class and the newly affluent, the Yiddishists and the Hebraists, the Zionists and the cultural nationalists" (Joselit 1993, p. 15). Summer camp was a particularly good fit for the Zionist youth movements—Young Judaea, Habonim Dror, Hashomer Hatsair, B'nei Akiva—who modeled their camps after the pioneering *kibbutzim* (collective settlements) in Israel. Zionist camping arrived on the scene in the 1930s and spread during the 1940s and 1950s. To this day, these camps maintain strong Zionist education, a preference for rustic living, and a kibbutz-like feel. This latter quality is enhanced by their relatively small size (an average of 230 beds versus an average of 308 for all other camps; see figure 2.2).

Denominational movement camps. The advent of the denominational movement camps after World War II marked a turning point in the Jewish camping movement. Sarna (2001) refers to this period as the "crucial decade in Jewish camping," the time when the field shifted from camps with social welfare or ideological aims to those with educational or religious missions. In 1947, the Conservative movement opened Camp Ramah in Wisconsin under the direction of the Jewish Theological Seminary (Cohen 1989; Dorph 1999; Fox 1997). That same year, the Reform movement opened its first camp, Camp Swig in California. Unlike the Ramah camps, the Reform movement camps have always been under the purview of the Union of American Hebrew Congregations (UAHC) and not the movement's seminary. During the 1950s, seven more denominational camps were established. By the summer of 2000, there were eighteen such camps (including one sponsored by the National Council of Synagogue Youth, the Orthodox youth movement) across the United States, from New England to the West Coast.

Prior to 1947, camping was a religiously pluralistic enterprise. The denominational movement camps, in contrast, were set up to promote a particular religious viewpoint. As educational arms of their movements, they all had—and continue to have—Jewish educators and rabbis on staff and formal Jewish learning sessions in the daily schedule. Chaim Potok was a division head at Camp Ramah in Pennsylvania's Pocono Mountains in the early 1950s. In his reminiscences, he ponders how staff managed to get through a camp day without collapsing from exhaustion. He writes, "We lived, it seemed to me, in a permanent state of exhilaration born of a sense of high purpose and accomplishment. We were educating the next generation of American Jews in a living Judaism" (Potok 1993, p. 7). Like the agency camps, the denominational camps were created to save lives. This time, however, the concerns were not about physical health and survival but about Jewish learning and the survival of American Jewry.

Private camps. Three types of camps included in our census are privately owned and operated: the non-Orthodox for-profit camps, the independent nonprofit camps, and the Orthodox private camps.

The first of these, the non-Orthodox for-profit Jewish camps, have had a significant and growing presence in the field of Jewish camping since the beginning of the twentieth century. While Jewish agencies were setting up charitable summer camps for needy children, private owners were setting up for-profit camps for the children of upper middle class Jewish families. In the 1920s and 1930s, camping increasingly became a middle class institution. This trend culminated in the exponential growth of private camps during the prosperous years after World War II. Today these camps dominate the field. About one in three of all Jewish residential camps are privately owned, non- or trans-denominational settings.

The first founded of the extant private for-profit camps is Androscoggin, a nondenominational boys camp established in Maine in 1907. Androscoggin, like some of the other camps in this category, meets only the minimum requirements for inclusion in our study. The current owners are Jewish, as are 80 percent of the campers. Although candles are lit on Friday night, the camp offers no explicit Jewish programming or education. Nonetheless, the camp considers itself a Jewish camp and many of the families that choose it for their children undoubtedly do so as well.

Blue Star Camps, founded by the Popkin family in 1948, represents another kind of for-profit (non-Orthodox) private camp. Over the years, the camp has remained true to its founding philosophy and purpose: "Individualized type camping based on the needs and interests of the campers, building self-confidence, self-respect and an understanding and appreciation of American and Jewish values while training for leadership and friendly, cooperative living within a group" (Popkin 1997, p. 9). Jewish values, it should be noted, do not dominate the camp's perspective but rather are given a place alongside American values. Nonetheless, the camp has never wavered in its Jewish identity. In a lively history of the camp, Herman Popkin tells of the time that "Uncle Newell," a Bunyanesque man from the hills of North Carolina, came to camp to apply for a position as caretaker. "Newell, you know that we're Jewish," Herman's brother Harry Popkin explained. "And that even though we have a policy of accepting everyone—black or white, and regardless of their religious beliefs—most of our children are of the same persuasion." "I know," Newel said. "Folks 'round here call you'uns the Jew camp" (Popkin 1997, p. 53). The camp community observes *Shabbat,* sings blessings at mealtimes, and enjoys kosher dining. Jewish education and Jewish cultural arts can also be found at Blue Star.

At one time, such private camps strove to have the "right" kind of camper. An early advertisement might emphasize a camp's "refined clientele," for example, (Joselit 1993), and the Jewish society page in the local press would carry the announcement of a young woman's departure to camp for the summer. To this day, these private camps, as evidenced by their relatively high tuitions and low levels of scholarship support, appear to be in a separate economic tier from the other camps (see table 2.7).

Fourteen of the camps in our scan of the landscape are designated as foundation or independent nonprofit camps. A few of these are run by philanthropic foundations. Most, however, are essentially private camps that, for financial reasons, have been incorporated as 501(c)3 nonprofit entities.

Another twelve camps are private Orthodox camps. Most of these are single-sex camps that offer an observant lifestyle for the summer, including kosher meals, daily prayers, and Jewish study. All of the private Orthodox camps in our census are located in the New York–New Jersey–Pennsylvania triangle. As noted earlier, many more such camps likely exist, but they could not be identified or persuaded to join the study.

Geography

The location of Jewish camps roughly matches the regional distribution of the Jewish population in the United States (cf. Goldstein 1992). The largest concentration of camps is in the Northeast, with two out of three Jewish camps located in New England and the New York–New Jersey–Pennsylvania triangle (figure 2.1). Market forces are undoubtedly at work. Not only are there more Jews in this area, but families here are also more likely to send their children to camp. Keysar, Kosmin, and Scheckner (2000), for example, found that 21 percent of Jewish children in New York ages ten to fourteen and 16 percent of those fifteen to seventeen went to Jewish summer camp in 1989 and 1990, compared with only half that proportion outside of New York. Although regional norms may contribute to this difference, it is clearly the case that children in New York have more close-to-home opportunities to participate in camp and more options from which to choose.

The concentration of camps in particular regions should not necessarily affect a child's access to a Jewish summer camp. Most camps draw from be-

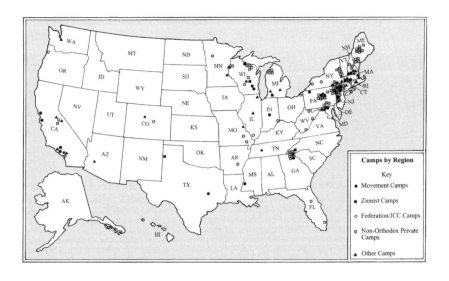

Region	Denominational movement	Zionist	JCC/Federation	Non-Orthodox private	Other	Total
New England (CT, MA, ME, NH, RI)	3	0	3	20	11	37
Northeast Triangle (NJ, NY, PA)	4	7	21	25	30	87
Other Mid-Atlantic (MD, TN, WV)	1	1	1	2	3	8
South/Southeast (FL, GA, MS, NC)	3	1	1	5	0	10
Midwest (IL, IN, MI, MN, MO, OH, WI)	3	4	6	10	7	30
West (AZ, CO, TX)	1	1	1	0	2	5
West Coast (CA, OR, WA)	3	1	2	2	6	14
Total	18	15	35	64	59	191

Figure 2.1. Camps by region.

yond their local communities and long-distance travel, even for young children, has become commonplace (table 2.2). Nonetheless, increased security concerns since the terrorist attacks of September 11, 2001, along with new fears about antisemitism, may give new relevance to the distance between home and camp. In the future, the simple question of distance may

Table 2.2. Extent of Camps' Geographic Draw

	Number of camps	Percentage
Local: draw primarily from within the state	35	23
Regional: draw mainly from within the region	42	28
Bi-regional: draw from two regions	46	30
National: draw most of their campers from three or more regions	29	19
Total	152	100

Note: Region was defined in accordance with the regional designations used in the National Jewish Population Survey. These also correspond with regional boundaries set by the U.S. Census.

become a more important factor both in parents' choices for their children and in the community's decisions about where to situate new camps.

Camps sponsored by local Jewish community centers or federations tend to draw their campers locally or from within their region. Those sponsored by the denominational movements generally draw their campers from one or two regions of the country. The camps that draw nationally are most often privately owned or sponsored by a Zionist movement or a community agency (table 2.3).

Not only does the prevalence of Jewish summer camps vary by region but so, too, does the culture of summer camping. For example, camps in the South frequently see children from communities whose Jewish population is smaller than that of the camp. This situation is less common in the Northeast, where many of the campers come from the major Jewish population centers of New York and Boston and their environs. In the Northeast, parents expect and accept four- or eight-week-long sessions. In the West, shorter sessions are the norm, with many children attending only one of several two- or three-week sessions offered throughout the summer. Both of these factors, in turn, influence how camps in these regions approach the task of Jewish socialization.

Camper Population
In order for a camp to be included in the census, at least 50 percent of its campers had to be Jewish. Most reported significantly higher percentages, resulting in an overall average of 95 percent (table 2.4). These camps thus

Table 2.3. Geographic Draw by Camp Type

Type of Camp	Local	Regional	Bi-regional	National	Total
Community					
Jewish federation/JCC	10	11	7	2	30
Agency/organization	8	4	3	6	21
Movement					
Zionist	3	2	4	4	13
Denominational	1	9	5	1	16
Private					
Non-Orthodox for-profit	9	10	25	12	56
Foundation/ independent nonprofit	3	6	2	2	13
Orthodox for-profit	1	0	0	2	3
Total	35	42	46	29	152

Table 2.4. Percentage of Jewish Campers by Camp Type

Type of camp	Average percentage of Jewish campers
Community	
Jewish federation/JCC	96
Agency/organization	99
Movement	
Zionist	100
Denominational	100
Private	
Non-Orthodox for-profit	89
Foundation/independent nonprofit	95
Orthodox for-profit	100
Overall	95

provide a Jewish social environment in which Jewish children live in a world comprised largely of their Jewish peers.

The number of campers also varies widely, a function of physical capacity, financial realities, market size, and owners' or sponsors' preferences. The smallest camp, an Orthodox *yeshiva* camp in New York, had just 35 campers in summer 2000, while the largest, an agency-sponsored camp in the Midwest, served 1,500 Jewish children. In all, one out of every four Jewish children attending a Jewish residential summer camp in the United States is at a non-Orthodox for-profit camp. The field's total capacity (i.e., total number of beds) is close to 58,000. Again, it should be noted that over one-third of these beds are in the non- or trans-denominational private camps (table 2.5).

On average, the denominational movements have built the largest camps and, indeed, in visiting them, one is often impressed by the sheer number of people sitting out on the hillside or filling the dining hall. In contrast, the Zionist movements have tended to build the smallest camps, ones that more often remind the visitor of a kibbutz in the *Yishuv* (prestate Israel; see figure 2.2).

As the field of Jewish summer camping celebrated its one hundredth anniversary, residential camps across the country were thriving. In the summer of 2000, the Jewish camps were, on average, filled to 96 percent capacity, with about half of the camps at full capacity. Many of the camps were fully enrolled early in the year and had a waiting list for other interested families. In order to gain a spot at some camps, parents needed to have signed up on visiting day the previous summer.

Overall, three-fourths of the campers are returnees from previous years. In practical terms, this means that directors have to "sell" only one-fourth of the available places at camp each year. The range is large, however, from a 20 percent return rate at a denominational movement camp to a 98 percent return rate at two private camps (figure 2.3). The importance of return rate should not be underestimated. Not only is a high return rate "good business," but it also means that camps have not just one summer in which to influence their campers, but sometimes as many as eight to ten years. Camp is the one institution in the community that seems to hold participants as they develop through childhood, to adolescence, to emerging adulthood. As Rabbi Sheldon Dorph, National Ramah

Table 2.5. Camp Capacity and Jewish Campers Served by Camp Type (rounded to nearest 100)

	Total number of camp beds	Total number of Jewish campers served
Community		
Jewish federation/JCC	10,200	17,000
Agency/organization	8,700	13,300
Movement		
Zionist	3,400	5,600
Denominational	7,000	12,400
Private		
Non-Orthodox for-profit	20,700	22,500
Foundation/independent nonprofit	4,100	7,700
Orthodox for-profit	3,600	4,400
Total	57,700	82,900

Note: Numbers are based on information provided by camp directors responding to the census survey. In cases of missing data, the average for the particular type of camp was used in estimating totals.

director, explained, "Within a given summer, the deepening of relationships, the processing of Jewish issues, the development of social skills, Jewish learning and physical skills are all enhanced geometrically by an extended eight-week summer. When this is multiplied over four to six years, we have added a half year of intensive experiential Judaism to a teenager's heart, mind, and soul. We are giving time to each learner to own his/her Jewishness—and that is the real power and magic of camp."[1]

Staff

Staff are essential members of the camp community who need to be considered a target audience in their own right. Significant numbers of Jewish professionals, including rabbis and teachers, come to camp each summer to "recharge." And large numbers of emerging adults, who might personally benefit from the Jewish life and education found at camp, are employed as counselors. Of the 18,000 Jewish young adults and Jewish professionals who work at a Jewish residential camp during the summer, the majority, just over 10,000, are counselors. Another 7,600 are directors, unit heads, educators, or support staff (table 2.6). Included in these num-

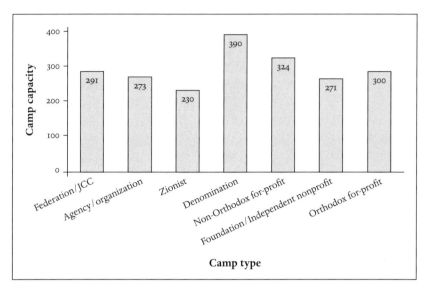

Figure 2.2. Camp capacity by camp type.

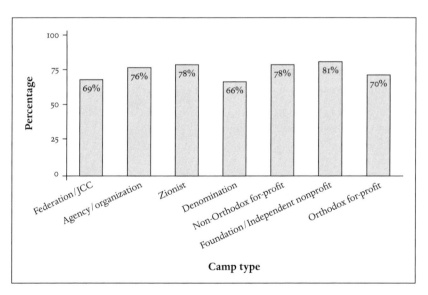

Figure 2.3. Percentage of campers returning from previous years.

Table 2.6. Number of Jewish Staff by Camp Type (rounded to nearest 100)

	Jewish bunk counselors	Other Jewish staff	Total Jewish staff
Community			
Jewish federation/JCC	2,100	1,500	3,600
Agency/organization	2,200	1,400	3,600
Movement			
Zionist	800	700	1,500
Denominational	1,300	1,400	2,700
Private			
Non-Orthodox for-profit	2,500	1,500	4,000
Foundation/independent nonprofit	700	400	1,100
Orthodox for-profit	800	700	1,500
Total (n = 191)	10,400	7,600	18,000

Note: Numbers are based on information provided by camp directors responding to the census survey. In cases of missing data, the average for the particular type of camp was used in estimating totals.

bers are an increasing number of Israelis, many of whom come to work at camp on short-term assignments as *shlichim* (emissaries) through the Jewish Agency. In summer 2000, this number totaled approximately 1,000. Two years later, the number of Israeli *shlichim* at American summer camps was over 1,200.

THE COST OF CAMP

Cost is a potentially important factor in whether families decide to send their children to summer camp. In summer 2000, the average tuition at a Jewish residential camp was about $625 per week or $2,500 for a month. As in all of the census data, there is a substantial range across camps. Two of the camps (a synagogue camp and a Chabad camp) charged less than $200 per week while thirteen camps charged $1,000 or more per week.

According to camp directors, just under 20 percent of the campers at Jewish overnight camps are on scholarship. On average, the Jewish camps spend only 6 percent of their budgets on camper support. Financially, the Jewish camping world is a two-tier system. As seen in table 2.7, the non-

Table 2.7. Cost by Camp Type

	Average weekly tuition	Average percentage of campers with scholarship	Average percentage of operating budget allocated to scholarships
Community			
Jewish federation/JCC	$514	25	6
Agency/organization	$510	37	21
Movement			
Zionist	$526	18	4
Denominational	$594	31	5
Private			
Non-Orthodox for-profit	$816	3	1
Foundation/independent nonprofit	$524	22	9
Orthodox for-profit	$453	25	13
Overall	$626	19	6

Orthodox for-profit private camps charge the highest fees, have the lowest percentage of campers with scholarships, and devote, on average, the least amount of their operating budgets to camper scholarships. The camps sponsored by agencies and organizations (including synagogues, Chabad, *yeshivot,* schools, etc.) not only charge the lowest tuition, but also support a significant percentage of campers who otherwise might not be able to attend summer camp.

JEWISH PRACTICES AT CAMP

The camp census was designed to show not only the physical size and shape of the field of Jewish camping but also its Jewish spirit. In order to document the extent to which the residential camps incorporate Jewish life and activities into their operations, the survey offered a checklist of seventeen ways that Judaism could be manifest at camp. Some of the items referred to religious practices (e.g., religious services or mealtime blessings), others to Jewish educational activities (e.g., Jewish cultural arts or *bar/bat mitzvah* tutoring), and still others to a connection to Israel (e.g., Israeli flag raising or Hebrew names for bunks).

Table 2.8. Percentage of Camps Incorporating Religious Practices by Camp Type

	Kosher meals	Daily prayers	Blessings at mealtimes
Community			
Jewish federation/JCC	97	29	94
Agency/organization	67	75	95
Movement			
Zionist	100	69	69
Denominational	59	100	100
Private			
Non-Orthodox for-profit	38	2	33
Foundation/independent nonprofit	93	36	86
Orthodox for-profit	100	100	100
Overall	68	38	70

Note: Data in this table are based on the 161 camps in the national census that provided information about their Jewish programming and activities.

Jewish residential camps of every type use mealtime as a focus of their efforts to create Jewish life (table 2.8). The majority of camps maintain a kosher kitchen and lead campers in blessings before and after meals. The low numbers for the non-Orthodox for-profit camps are most salient. On this dimension, as in every other dimension on the checklist, they are the least likely to design their programs to incorporate Jewish practices and activities.

The highlight of the week at camp is *Shabbat.* Most days at camp follow from one to the next in an indistinguishable flow. But *Shabbat* stands out as a special day, different from all the others. The full observance of *Shabbat* would include Friday evening services, candle lighting, and a special meal with *challah* (braided bread) and wine or grape juice; Saturday morning services; and a Saturday evening *Havdalah* service that marks the end of the Sabbath with blessings, song, candlelight, and the sweet smell of spices. All of the denominational movement camps and the private Orthodox camps observe *Shabbat* from Friday night candle lighting through *Havdalah* (table 2.9). Many of the other camps also ob-

Table 2.9. Percentage of Camps Incorporating Shabbat Practices by Camp Type

	Friday evening			Saturday	
	Religious services	Special meal	Candle lighting	Morning services	*Havdalah* service
Community					
Jewish federation/JCC	94	97	97	97	97
Agency/organization	95	100	100	95	95
Movement					
Zionist	92	100	100	79	100
Denominational	100	100	100	100	100
Private					
Non-Orthodox for-profit	58	49	65	18	11
Foundation/independent nonprofit	86	86	86	79	71
Orthodox for-profit	100	100	100	100	100
Overall	81	80	86	66	65

Note: Data in this table are based on the 161 camps in the national census that provided information about their Jewish programming and activities.

serve *Shabbat,* although clearly they give more attention to Friday night than to Saturday.

A majority of the camps in our census offer some form of Jewish education, broadly defined in the survey as formal or informal study sessions or educational activities. Table 2.10 shows a now-familiar pattern. A majority of the Jewish residential camps, but very few of the non-Orthodox private camps offer Jewish educational activities. The one exception to this pattern is *bar/bat mitzvah* training, which is found equally at the religious camps and at the non- or trans-denominational private camps. The private camps, it should be remembered, were established as businesses intent on being financially independent and, if successful, turning a profit. Sarna (2001) believes that, historically, the profit motive is implicated in the slow development of the educational component of Jewish camping. He notes that

Table 2.10. Percentage of Camps Incorporating Jewish Educational and Cultural Activities by Camp Type

	Jewish cultural arts	Jewish education	Bar/bat mitzvah training	Jewish values incorporated into activities
Community				
Jewish federation/JCC	97	77	80	91
Agency/organization	95	90	84	85
Movement				
Zionist	100	100	77	100
Denominational	100	100	88	100
Private				
Non-Orthodox for-profit	19	9	84	16
Foundation/ independent nonprofit	86	64	86	71
Orthodox for-profit	100	100	100	100
Overall	69	58	84	64

Note: Data in this table are based on the 161 camps in the national census that provided information about their Jewish programming and activities.

owner-investors feared that if camp were too much like school, then campers would not want to return, and the investment would be lost. Such a sentiment can still be found among some camp owners today.

Finally, many Jewish educators see great value in connecting summer camp with an Israel experience. Campers are likely candidates for teen Israel trips. Rabbi Allan Smith, long-time director of the Youth Division of the Union of American Hebrew Congregations, says that the Reform movement's teen trips to Israel did not attract large numbers of participants until they made the connection with the camp community.[2] Moreover, with Israel trip enrollment numbers virtually pegged to security in the Middle East, rising and falling with current events, there is a need to find alternative venues for imparting Zionist/Israel education and transmitting a love of Israel. Summer camps are an obvious place in which to fulfill this need.

Table 2.11. Percentage of Camps Incorporating Israel/Zionist Activities by Camp Type

	Israeli Flag/ *Hatikvah*	Hebrew names for places and activities	Israel trip for older campers
Community			
Jewish federation/JCC	71	57	34
Agency/organization	58	79	21
Movement			
Zionist	100	100	62
Denominational	88	94	88
Private			
Non-Orthodox for-profit	4	2	0
Foundation/independent nonprofit	79	57	36
Orthodox for-profit	50	75	0
Overall	50	48	28

Note: Data in this table are based on the 161 camps in the national census that provided information about their Jewish programming and activities.

The data shown in table 2.11 were gathered during a time of relative peace in the Middle East. Even in normal times, few non-movement camps offer an Israel experience for older campers or counselors-in-training. Nonetheless, Israel is often remembered at camp with the presence of the Israeli flag and the singing of the Israeli national anthem, *Hatikvah,* at flag raising. Other representations of Israel, not included in the census, are also common at the Jewish residential camps: Israeli counselors, *Yom Yisrael* (Israel Day; a day of Israeli food, games, and learning), Israeli posters and maps hanging on the walls of the dining hall, and so on.

PERSPECTIVES ON THE LANDSCAPE

What stands out from the national census of Jewish residential camps is the complexity of the system of camps that have been built over the past century by and for the American Jewish community. Both structurally and programmatically, the variety among Jewish camps is vast. There are non-denominational private camps and camps organized by the religious movements. There are East Coast camps and West Coast camps, old camps and camps newly built, camps that create small communities during the summer with fifty campers and those that create small cities with five hundred campers. There are camps that cost $200 per week and camps that cost $1,000 per week. And, most importantly for assessing the role of camps in socializing children as members of the Jewish people, there are camps with minimal Jewish programming and those in which Jewish life and education pervade the entire day.

Although community leaders bemoan the small percentage of the youth population attending Jewish camps, the fact is that Jewish camps touch the lives of tens of thousands—perhaps as many as 100,000—children and teens each summer. These campers are joined by nearly 20,000 adults who work at camp. Many of these staff members are emerging adults who are on an exploration of their own identities and life possibilities. Each year, roughly 20,000 new Jewish campers come into camp along with perhaps 10,000 new Jewish staff members. In this way, the number of American Jews who have been exposed to Jewish experiences and learning at camp continually grows.

Also striking about the numbers is the dominance of the non-Orthodox private camps and the challenge they pose to the organized Jewish community. These camps reach the greatest number of children, but they are also the ones that least often engage in Jewish practices or provide Jewish education. They are independent entities with great flexibility in determining what kind of Jewish environment and what types of education and ritual practices they will offer. However, as profit-driven businesses, they may not be open to changes that would enhance their potential as Jewish socializing agents.

As we noted in chapter 1, camps are effective socializing agents because they create the kind of environment and encourage the kinds of relationships that are most likely to lead to social learning. The census provides few clues as to how they accomplish these tasks. How do Jewish camps—in just a few weeks in the summer—work their magic, particularly in an era when secular culture is dominant, assimilation normative, and family life often disengaged from that of the Jewish community? To address this question, we need to take a close-up, inside look at camps. The next chapter, "Camp is Camp," moves us from census numbers to camp stories, from a bird's-eye view of the field to an on-the-ground examination of Jewish camping.

3

Camp Is Camp

Jewish tradition says that the study of Torah is equal to all of the other *mitzvot* (commandments) because it leads to them all. So, too, is fun equal to all of the other purposes of camp because it leads to them all. In general terms, these purposes are defined as the mental, physical, social, and spiritual growth of each camper (American Camping Association 1997). In particularistic terms, these purposes also include immersing children in Jewish life, inspiring them to greater identification with the Jewish people, and instilling in them the joy of Judaism. This chapter, based on our participant-observation study, explains how camp's power as a Jewish socializing agent is derived from its dedication to fun.

In order to understand how camps work their magic, during summer 2000 we became participant observers at eighteen Jewish camps across the United States, in the Northeast, South, and West. Within each region, camps were selected to represent a range of sponsors: the religious movements, Zionist organizations, communities, foundations, and private ownership (table 3.1). The purpose of these visits was to observe and document the varieties of Jewish life at camp. We came to camp as participant observers and, based on a carefully designed protocol, collected a wealth of data about life in each camp.

Each site visit lasted three or four days and, in almost all cases, included *Shabbat*. The protocol for the visits included observation of everyday activ-

Table 3.1. Camp Site Visits

	Northeast	South	West
Conservative		1	1
Reform	3	1	1
JCC	2	1	1
Zionist	2	1	
Foundation	1		1
Private	1	1	

Note: Inclusion of all types of camps in each region was not feasible. For example, it was not possible to identify a Zionist camp in the West or a foundation camp in the South.

ities, participation in *t'fillot* (daily prayers) and *Shabbat* observance, individual or group interviews with key players (director, assistant director, educators, *shlichim,* specialists, unit heads, bunk counselors), and a review of curricula, songbooks, training manuals, parent information packets, and other camp literature. We did not formally gather information from campers. Human subject regulations, which we adhere to as university-based researchers, require special consent to gather data from minors. Rather than ask parents for permission to interview their children, we limited data collection to observation of public behavior. Although campers would approach us to ask questions about why we were at camp and to explain what they were doing, all of our systematic data gathering is based on observation, staff input, and written materials.

As participant observers, our days and nights were spent walking around camp; sitting in on activities; participating in sports, prayers, and mealtime rituals; and speaking with staff. Armed with notebooks and tape recorders, we kept running accounts of our observations, experiences, and conversations during the week. *Shabbat* observations were entered on Saturday night after *Havdalah.* Notes and tapes were later translated into over two hundred pages of field notes. These notes are replete with stories of success and failure in capturing the Jewish imagination of children at camp.

PURPOSE OF CAMP

"Camp is camp" are the director's first words after greeting us at the gate. His aphorism, intended to set the framework for our visit, instructs us to think of camp as the canvas upon which Jewish life is painted. Like any Jewish camp director, he understands the primacy of camp. He knows that he must attend to all of the features that make camp a camping experience before he can attend to those that make camp a Jewish experience. As another camp director explained, "It's got to be an intensive Jewish environment . . . but it had better be exciting, warm, caring, positive. It's got to be the greatest place in the world that they've ever been, or it's not going to click."

Virtually every camp's website, advertisements, and brochure emphasize similar themes: that the camp is safe and nurturing, that its campers have opportunities to grow and to make new friends, that camp is fun. In camp surveys, parents say that the most important benefits their children derive from camp are personal (increased self-confidence and self-esteem), social (making new friends, learning how to get along with others), and recreational (gaining an appreciation for nature and the outdoors, learning recreational skills) (cf. Marsh 2000).

Camps that are intentional about promoting the personal benefits of camping and explicitly state so in their camp philosophy appear, in fact, to do a better job of helping children increase their self-confidence and self-esteem. And, as the research consistently finds, this higher self-regard correlates with developmental outcomes: more positive relationships with peers and parents, greater satisfaction with life, higher academic achievement, more responsible attitude toward sexual behavior, and more positive adjustment during the middle-school transition (Marsh 2000). Seen this way, camping does seem to have magical power.

Personal growth objectives notwithstanding, the fundamental purpose of camp is to have fun. In this regard, camp stands in sharp contrast to school (which may be fun, but is unlikely to profess fun as a core tenet). When campers have fun, they are more likely to enjoy the personal, social, and recreational benefits of camp. In the spirit of fun, they are more likely to take advantage of opportunities to take risks, experiment with new behaviors, make friends, and learn new skills. Furthermore, when campers have fun, they return year after year. The return rate has several benefits. A high return rate ensures that the camp can focus more on its program and less on advertising and marketing. One director gave us a specific number—he needs a 75 percent return rate in order to remain financially viable. A high return rate gives endurance to a community that must be recreated every year. Returning campers strengthen the camp community by identifying as members of the community, as people who belong there and "own" the place. Most importantly, a high return rate magnifies the camp's potential to influence a child's development. Children who return to camp year after year are more likely to benefit from camp's lessons than are those who attend for just a few weeks in one season.

INGREDIENTS THAT CREATE CAMP MAGIC

Our observations confirm a good deal of common wisdom about camps. Camps have their own peculiar lifestyle, no doubt a function of what is now referred to in the vernacular as a "24/7" environment. Decades ago, social psychologist Kurt Lewin (1947) wrote about the use of group experiences to effect personal and social change. He noted that the effectiveness of camps to change ideology or behaviors depends in part on the possibility of their creating "cultural islands." The stronger the accepted subculture of the camp and the more isolated it is, he wrote, the more it will minimize resistance to change. In fact, the camps we studied isolate children from their normal environment and envelop them in an enclosed society. Most of the camps we visited were a far cry from the idealized image of the rugged, pitch-in-and-do-it-yourself kind of camp. Yet, even with shoe bags filled with expensive shoes, hair dryers, and CD players in the bunks, camp is very different from home. From our observations, several qualities define summer camp and are responsible for what Lewin refers to as "change" and workers in the field often refer to as camp "magic."

Isolated Setting

All of the camps in our study are in rural or exurban settings and offer outdoor living surrounded by natural beauty. Most of the camps we visited are distant from the campers' hometowns and, to get to them, one has to drive for miles through the countryside. We visited camps that sit in the mountains and those that are nestled into coves of lakes or tucked away in the woods by a river. Geographically and perceptually, these camps are removed from the rest of the world. Even camps that are close to major highways feel isolated once you arrive and become engrossed in the camp community.

Camps promote the sense of isolation by creating separation between camp and home, between camp time and school time. Separation is achieved not only through the distinctive features of camp life, but also through barriers the camp erects against the outside world. For example, parents' access to the camp is controlled (generally restricted to visiting day), campers' use of the telephone is prohibited or limited, and campers' exposure to newspapers, radio, television, and the Internet is minimized.[1] Camps are physically laid out to give the sense of being in a world apart; there is little or no awareness of the outside world. One camp is concerned that motorists, passing by on an isolated rural road, could catch a glimpse of the camp from the road. A staff member at another camp complains that she can hear cars passing by at night. This camp, too, is located on a lone country road. Camps have low tolerance for any intrusion.

In this Brigadoon-like place, time and space are compressed. Everyone seems to live in the here-and-now. As a result, campers move quickly into camp mode when they arrive. A sense of community forms virtually overnight. Much like Sherif and Sherif's boys, participants quickly bond with one another, and everyone soon enters into the rhythm of camp life. Despite our expectations to the contrary, the intensity of camp erases obvious differences between camps with two- or three-week programs and those with programs of longer duration.

Separated from the outside world, camps can create *physically safe* environments in which campers may roam widely and freely. For many campers, such freedom is not possible in their home communities. Several camps we visited have security guards posted at the camp gate (in two cases, twenty-four hours per day), adding to the sense of security felt by both the campers and their parents. Other camps have electric gates at their front entrances that can be opened only with a security code. Separated from the outside world, camps can also create *emotionally safe* environments that encourage campers to take risks and try new experiences. Camp, more than school, lets children discover and explore their interests and talents. At one camp, for example, there were tryouts for a team for which only a few campers would be chosen. It was surprising to see a large number try out, including many who had no chance of succeeding. Repeatedly at the camps we visited, we saw children who "could not sing" get up on stage and sing, children who "could not dance" dance, and children who "could not play" a particular sport join in the game.

Total Environment

Campers are at camp twenty-four hours a day, seven days a week. They eat, sleep, play, learn, and work in this environment. So self-contained is the environment that camps set their clocks and calendars as they wish. The end of *Shabbat* is traditionally when three stars are visible in the sky. One camp sets the clock back one hour so that *Shabbat* will end early enough to permit Saturday evening programming. Another moved the observance of *Tishah B'Av* up one day because the holiday would otherwise have fallen on the night of the final banquet.[2] Still other camps celebrate Hanukkah in July or Purim in August.

In a total environment, problems and differences cannot be escaped but must be worked out. For campers, there is no going home at the end of the day, no vacations from camp, no weekends off. The director of an independent camp enumerated the lessons to be learned in such a total environment: "To have to duke it out with cabin mates, to learn with each other what it means to cooperate, to compromise, to communicate clearly, to put your ego away when you don't get your way, to learn to live with someone you know you're never going to like but the adults are saying you have to be respectful toward—those are really important skills, important for us to teach. And deep down the kids know they're important for them to learn."

Community

Perhaps the most important feature of summer camps is the way in which they create a temporary community that springs up phoenix-like each year in June and closes down by the end of August. It is an intentional community, which means that attention is paid to fostering the relationships and spirit that make the camp a tightly-knit whole. Such intentionality is seen in camp tee-shirts, all-camp songfests, inter-camp rivalries, and the exaltation of camp traditions. For all intents and purposes, camp is a uni-generational community—a world of children, teens, and college students, with just enough older adults to manage the system.

Regardless of whether camps emphasize individual achievement or group activities, they all place great importance on social relations, friendship formation, and community building. The bunk, where campers live with their peers, is the central social and organizational structure at camp. It is this structure, probably more than anything else, which develops self-reliance and teamwork, and teaches campers how to get along with others. Counselors who live in the bunks fulfill every adult role vis-à-vis the campers, from teacher to "cool" big brother or sister. Campers spend more time with and have more access to their counselors at camp than they do with their parents at home. Through bunk life and the intensity of camp, they develop a deep intimacy with bunkmates, counselors, and other staff.

For us, the community aspect of Jewish camps highlighted key differences between supplementary religious school and camp. With rare exceptions, religious schools pay scant attention to community building and group bonding, and offer few opportunities in which these might occur spontaneously (eating together, solving problems together, staying overnight together). Supplementary religious schools are "adult environments," located in the synagogue that the parents (not the children) have joined. Differential attitudes toward religious school versus camp may emanate from young people's strong affection for community, team spirit, and friendship.

Camp Culture

Finally, each camp is a society with its own culture. Culture here is used in the anthropological sense. It includes language, norms, values, customs, traditions, history, mythology, and symbols. At camp, the loudspeaker becomes the *"taksheevu* (attention) machine"; the group of counselor assistants becomes a secret society with rumors of a hot tub in their special space; and the winners of color wars become heroes.

Camps tend to be strongly traditional institutions, passing on rituals and customs from one generation of campers to the next. At one of the movement camps, we were privy to the return of the oldest campers from a five-day whitewater rafting trip. This homecoming, we learned, is a longstanding celebratory tradition at camp. The oldest campers smear themselves with wet mud immediately prior to their grand, whooping entrance into the packed dining hall. During this entrance, they dramatically hug younger campers, sharing their mud and exuberance. They do endless cheers, are placed center stage, and accorded high status in front of the whole community. The previous night, we had been with the fifth and sixth grade boys, who were anticipating the return of the older group, imagining themselves one day being on the long overnight, and also excitedly wondering if they would get muddied by the returning heroes.

At another camp, the strength of tradition was affirmed by the cook who was rebuked by the director for serving hot dogs for lunch one Monday. The cook should have known better. The traditional Monday lunch at that camp is, and will always be, grilled cheese sandwiches. Traditions are so strong that the boys at yet another camp eagerly await the year they will be old enough to dance in skirts. Such is the power of camp tradition that it can transform a behavior that would cause embarrassment in the outside world into an honor in the camp world.

CAMP AND JUDAISM

The same ingredients that make camp work as a special place and as an agent for healthy development also make it work as an institution that motivates and educates Jewishly. The fun of camp makes campers open and available to Jewish practices that they might otherwise ignore or reject. There is an intensity to Jewish life at summer camp. As one counselor noted, "You see the entire Jewish lifecycle at camp. In a month, you deal with every single theme that you'd go through in a lifetime." The separation of camp from the outside world and the close-knit quality of the camp community make it possible to live Judaism at camp in a holistic fashion. Judaism is lived as a matter of course and takes no extraordinary effort. "Judaism is natural at camp," a counselor at an observant camp told us. "*Minyan* (praying in a group) is what you do. You don't have to give up anything to do a Jewish life when you're at camp." The pace of camp and the warm, slow days of summer allow for an easy approach to Jewish teaching. "You can do it gently, slowly," said the director of an Orthodox private camp.

The match between what camping offers and what is needed to create a compelling Jewish youth world is striking. Equally striking, however, are the curious juxtapositions that can result from the blend: A dining room full of campers begins the blessing after meals. It quickly becomes a spirited cheer replete with stomping, banging, and clapping. The whole camp gathers at the flagpole, showered and dressed for *Shabbat*. Voices rise in song—first a popular rock song, then *Hatikvah*. Instead of a *d'var Torah* (Torah commentary) during *Shabbat* services, counselors put on a *parashah* (weekly Torah portion) play, often a humorous skit with a Jewish message. After *Shabbat* morning services, campers congregate at the lakefront for a beach party with a disk jockey. In all these instances, the campers seem unaware of where Judaism leaves off and the American aspects of camp begin. As in Fishman's (2000) description of the coalescence of American and Jewish values, the lines are not simply blurred; they are confused. This easy co-existence of the Jewish and the American, the sacred and the profane, is perhaps a more curious outcome of the marriage of Jewish education and camping.

CAMP STANDARDS VERSUS JEWISH PROGRAMMING

Summer camps are subject to myriad local and state regulations regarding health and safety. In addition, all of the camps we visited are members of and accredited by the American Camping Association (ACA). Many of them proudly display the ACA logo at their entrance. ACA sets the standard for camping in the United States, whether the camps are Jewish, Christian, or nonsectarian. ACA-accredited camps have met or exceeded nearly three hundred standards that address every detail of camp from the director's background, to preparation and storage of food, to the qualifications of medical personnel and professional staff (see table 3.2). Additional standards apply to aquatics, horseback riding, and travel programs. ACA standards are recognized by courts of law and by government regulators as *the* national standards of the camp industry. They are designed to assure that "camp provides a supervised, positive environment with controlled boundaries to help children grow." Camps go through a rigorous review process every three years in order to maintain their ACA accreditation.

Regardless of how well a Jewish camp delivers on its Jewish promise, the ACA guidelines are the minimum standards that it must meet in order to remain viable. Before a camp can consider what level of *kashrut* (Jewish di-

Table 3.2. ACA Accreditation Standards

Camp function	Standards
Site/food service	Fire protection, maintenance, sleeping areas, bathing/toilet facilities, food service areas and practices
Transportation	Driver and vehicle requirements, traffic control, transportation safety
Health care	Staff and facility requirements, medication management, required health information and record keeping
Management	Safety and security regulations, staff emergency training, crisis communications, insurance, planning
Staffing	Staff qualifications, training, ratios, supervision and behavior management guidelines
Program	Goals for camper development, orientation and safety policies for general and specialized programs (including aquatics, challenge course, trips, and horseback riding)

From the American Camping Association. 1998. *Accreditation Standards for Camp Programs and Services.* Martinsville, Ind.: American Camping Association.

etary laws) it will observe, it needs to be certain that its food service meets basic health and safety requirements. As we saw on our site visits, camps may compromise on *kashrut,* but they cannot compromise on sanitation. Unclean kitchens (in the secular sense) will be shut down by the authorities.

Driven by health and safety concerns, we repeatedly saw camps compromise on Jewish teachings. For example, many Jewish camps, which exist in the great and awesome beauty of nature, have begun to talk about environmentalism from a Jewish perspective. They teach that we are *shomrim,* protectors or guardians of the earth, which God has placed in our charge. These same Jewish camps, however, violate ecological principles in their everyday operations. When a camp noted for its model *teva* (nature) program built a new kitchen, it did not install a dishwasher because washing dishes always leaves soap residue, a common cause of stomach disorders. As a result, the camp uses disposable plastic- and paperware in the dining room and discards daily mountains of waste materials that are neither reusable nor recyclable.

National leadership of the movement camps holds certain expectations for Jewish practices. At a camp where *kipot* (skullcaps) are expected to be worn at daily prayers and at meals, we noticed that few of the boys had their heads covered. Why, we asked, was a simple Jewish norm being violated? As a camp leader explained, the boys often forget to bring their *kipot* with them, so the camp provides a bin of *kipot* outside the dining room and the chapel. With an outbreak of head lice moving rapidly through camp, there was no choice—the bins had to be removed.

At religiously observant camps, morning prayers, in accordance with Jewish tradition, are to be said before eating. One such camp, however, has its older campers *daven Shacharit* (pray the morning service) after breakfast. Jewish law notwithstanding, camp leaders find that their teenagers have difficulty rising early and that the quality of their prayer experience increases significantly with more rest and a full stomach.

As these examples testify, it is not possible to remove the Jewish management of camp from the operational management of camp. When a Jewish lesson confronts a common health issue, the campers' well-being trumps Judaism. Only after the camp has met its commitment to provide a safe, healthy, nurturing environment can it turn its attention to meeting its promise to provide a rich and meaningful Jewish experience.

Campers come to camp to have fun. But once there, they also have a chance to encounter Judaism through *Shabbat* observance and simple matters of daily life, through formal study sessions and informal educational activities. Given the all-encompassing nature of the camping experience and the possibility of suffusing the very atmosphere with Judaism, camp may transmit Jewish values and skills in an organic fashion. To understand this process, in the next chapter we turn to the varieties of informal and formal Jewish education found at camp.

4

Candy, Not Castor Oil

JEWISH EDUCATION AT CAMP

It is a Jewish tradition to give children candy when they study Torah so that they will associate the sweetness of the candy with the sweetness of Torah. The educational theory of summer camping is similar: If children come to associate Jewish life with sweetness—the smell of pine trees, the closeness of friends, laughter in the bunk—what they practice and learn at camp will remain with them for a lifetime. As described by a senior staff member of an observant camp, *Birkat Ha'mazon* (grace after meals) becomes associated with "being in the most wonderful place in the world with their best friends." This association "sticks" and "builds inside them," he continued, "so that they later, often post-college, want to get it back, to recapture it. They seek that out. They try to find communities where they can get that same feeling. They go looking for it." According to staff across the spectrum of camp types, the claim that the camp/Judaism association can change the trajectory of children's lives is both realistic and based on sound educational theory.

Camps, as settings for informal education, treat Jewish education very differently than do religious schools. Fun, as described earlier, is the first principle of camp and it is also the key to camp's approach to Jewish education. Some camps are proud of how they present Judaism to their campers without "ramming it down their throats." The philosophy of one such camp, for example, is to allow each camper and counselor to come to Judaism on his or her own terms: "What we offer Jewishly is very much a buffet—you take whatever appeals to you, nothing will be forced. If you stand back and let children snack goods that they want, they're probably going to love the product. So with everything—it's a banquet, it's a party." The notions of Jewish life as a party and Jewish choices as a banquet are not generally found in the corridors of religious and day schools.

Jewish socialization at camp takes place through formal and informal Jewish educational activities as well as through everyday interactions among campers, counselors, and educators. In this way, learning takes place both at appointed times when the group gathers for *limud* (Jewish learning) and at any moment during the day when the individual learner is ready. When it comes to particulars, each camp has its own approach to Jewish teaching. Some have explicit Jewish education only one hour a week; others have daily *shiurim* (lessons). Some focus on religious text and practices, others on Israel and Zionism, and still others on Jewish culture and values. Whatever the focus, educational activities are tailored to the campers' age and their developmental stage. Camps also differ in terms of their educational goals, the degree to which they integrate Jewish education into their program, the extent to which they spread responsibility for education among all staff, and the relative emphasis they place on formal or informal educational activities.

EDUCATIONAL GOALS

A camp's goals for Jewish education are shaped by the camp's sponsorship, leadership, population, and history. As a result, we found the goals, as articulated by the directors and educators, to be as diverse as the camps themselves. Here are examples from each of the different types of camps in our sample:

COMMUNITY CAMP. The director at a Jewish community center camp says that the priority at this camp is to make Judaism "fun." The approach, therefore, is to offer "opportunities" for Jewish practice but not to push them, and to emphasize respect for differences in religious orientation and practice.

ZIONIST MOVEMENT CAMP. At a camp sponsored by a Zionist organization, the emphasis is on informal education that is fun. Every activity at camp is connected to Israel, cultural Judaism, or leadership. So strong is the educational focus of this camp that controversy erupted when the camp invested in night lighting for the basketball and tennis courts. Some leaders questioned the appropriateness of the expenditure because it did not contribute directly to the camp's Zionist mission.

CONSERVATIVE MOVEMENT CAMP. According to the director of a Ramah camp we visited, the camp is "an educational institution, not just a recreational institution," and the majority of the campers come from families who are "committed to Jewish education." As a result, the camp unambivalently assigns an important role in its program to formal Jewish education.

REFORM MOVEMENT CAMP. Asserting that camp is mainly about "doing Jewish things with Jewish people," the director of this camp emphasizes the social aspects of the camping experience over the formal educational aspects. His view is supported by a national leadership that values the role of camping in "creating Jewish memories."

PRIVATE NONPROFIT CAMP. The director defines this camp as a "Jewish cultural camp." The premise of the Jewish program is that Judaism is "not something you study at camp; it's something you do." Rather than formal Jewish education classes, the camp holds regular group discussions on life values and ethical behavior.

ORTHODOX PRIVATE CAMP. The implicit mission of this camp is to foster Jewishness by giving campers a sense of Jewish pride and respect for Judaism. Believing that "*Yiddishkeit* (Jewishness) begins with *menschlichkeit* (being a good person)," the director places a strong emphasis on character development. One of the most effective aspects of the camp's Jewish programming is "*Midot* (character traits) of the Day."

The leadership of every Jewish camp establishes the camp's Jewish purpose. It tries to align its program with that purpose and attracts campers whose families accept that purpose. Various approaches thus co-exist in the field of Jewish summer camping. Some are grounded in Jewish text, others in Zionism, cultural Judaism, or Jewish values. While some camps place their Jewish purpose at the center of their overall mission, others hold it on the periphery. Every director and educator we encountered was able to articulate clear goals, but not all camps were able to implement their full vision. At some of these camps in summer 2000, there was a palpable sense of striving and obvious attempts to find new ways to engage campers in Jewish life.

INTEGRATION OF JEWISH EDUCATION

One of the fault lines between vision and implementation is found in the integration of Jewish education into camp life. In some cases, Jewish education is relegated to specific compartments in the camp day, while in other cases, it is seamlessly woven into the very fabric of camp. Where Jewish education is compartmentalized, it is seen as an activity like any other, fit into the schedule along with swimming, rocketry, and arts and crafts. Where Jewish learning is infused into any and all activities, campers are as likely to encounter Jewish education on the high ropes course as they are in *limud*. Although a camp may be inclined toward one programming philosophy or the other, we found evidence of both at every camp we visited.

Compartmentalization

Some educators consider the compartmentalization model "inauthentic" Jewish education. Admittedly, we experienced several jarring disjunctions that resulted from compartmentalization. For example, at one camp, we sat in on a Holocaust education class where eight- to ten-year-olds listened to a presentation by a rabbi and a Holocaust survivor. We were shaken from our own involvement when the session ended, even before there was time for questions, and the children ran off to free swim.

Furthermore, we saw how compartmentalization can constrain the amount of time available for Jewish education. One camp decided to offer an informal discussion group, "Rap with the Rabbi," as a *chug* (elective activity). The rabbi thought it would be an educator's dream come true, but the administration "set the program up for failure" by scheduling it opposite one of the campers' favorite activities. Such dynamics are more likely to occur when Judaism is confined to a box.

These critiques notwithstanding, a compartmentalized program may work for certain kinds of camps. At one of the secular Jewish camps, Judaism has always been highly contained, and there is little interest in infusing it into everyday activities. Formal Jewish education is restricted to the "culture class," in which each bunk, twice a week, meets in the lounge with the camp's Jewish educator. They talk about a wide range of topics related to everyday life, relationships, values and, tangentially, Judaism. The class is highly popular. "At any other camp," the educator noted, "culture class would be the first thing a camper would skip. But not here." We observed two of the classes, fascinated with the campers' engagement and level of participation. They adore the teacher and call him "*Abba*" (Daddy). They approach him constantly—after class, in the dining hall, wherever they see him—to talk to him and ask him questions. During the school year, we later learned, dozens of campers continue their conversations with him via e-mail.

This class seems to work because it is an ingrained component of the camp's program in which every camper expects to take part. It is led by a beloved figure, someone with whom campers will discuss things they probably would not mention to their parents. The content of the class has high personal relevance, dealing with the campers' personal beliefs, values, and behaviors. The class is downtime from the fast-paced camp day—a chance to "hang out," eat candy, talk, and listen. It has no curriculum, no structure, no tests, no right or wrong answers. Nearly everything the participants say is validated by the educator. After he reads an allegorical story to the group, he asks for reactions. When one girl insists that she "doesn't get it," the leader says, "How great it is that we're here together trying to figure it out!" Even failure to understand is validated as worthwhile.

Integration

Jewish education, second only to the safety and welfare of the camp community, is the core of the Conservative movement camps we visited. The Ramah camping experience is focused and shaped by Jewish learning (through prayer, study, ritual, customs, cultural activities) and by living within a community bound by Jewish law. At these camps, it is virtually impossible to separate the secular from the sacred. Jewish values and ethics are taught on the soccer field and *Shabbat* morning Torah readings are assigned at an evening campfire program. Other camps, too, are moving toward a more integrated approach to Jewish education "so that the block of time with the Jewish programmer isn't the only time we're doing something Jewish."

When integration is pursued, Jewish learning has the potential to be infused into many different activities. Across various types of camps, for example, we observed children in arts and crafts making *kipot,* painting *mezuzot,* and making *Eshet Chayil* spoons to present to their mothers on visiting day.[1] One camp's special fine arts program begins each day with the presentation of a Jewish text that sets the theme for the day or provides an inspirational starting point for the creative process. In singing sessions at another camp, the campers seamlessly move from folk songs, to modern Israeli popular songs, to Hebrew songs—all sung with easy familiarity and enthusiasm.

The theater program at one camp puts on a production of *Children of Eden,* a playful musical about the Garden of Eden, Noah, and the flood. At another camp, the drama specialist engages the children in exercises designed to reflect Jewish values. At still another camp, where the director urged specialists to incorporate more Judaic content, the drama teacher stages the Cinderella wedding scene under a traditional Jewish *chupah* (wedding canopy).

Jewish learning infuses the outdoor programs as well. On an overnight in a nearby forest, campers learn how to start a fire, how to pitch a tent, and how to prepare kosher meals over the campfire. Another outdoor education program includes nature appreciation and awareness games. The campers learn how and why to say the blessings for plants, animals, and rainbows. They play *tikkun olam* games.[2] And they tell Jewish stories around the campfire at bedtime.

Every attempt at integration does not succeed. At one camp, for example, the opportunity to make traditional Jewish objects in arts and crafts had little meaning for the children. The arts and crafts director, a non-Jew, did not know how to make the creative process meaningful in a Jewish sense. In other situations, we saw attempts to use Jewish principles to resolve conflicts fall flat. Gaga, Israeli dodge ball, is a popular game at some Jewish camps because it does not require a fixed number of players and in no way favors the skills of boys over those of girls. The object of the game, often played in a small circular pit, is to avoid having the ball touch your leg. Disputes inevitably arise over whether or not a player has been touched. In the heat of a contested Gaga match, attempts by counselors to apply Jewish values to conflict resolution have little impact.

CENTRALIZATION OF JEWISH EDUCATION

The extent to which the Judaics program is compartmentalized or integrated influences who is assigned the responsibility for Jewish education. Where Jewish education is compartmentalized, it is centralized in the hands of specialists: rabbis, Jewish educators, Israeli *shlichim*. Where Jewish education is integrated, responsibility for it is shared by specialists and bunk counselors. The ability to integrate Judaics is largely a function of the skill and background of the staff. It is also a reflection of the camp's sense of its Jewish purpose.

Centralization

One day, the rabbi at a denominational movement camp taught the blessing to say upon seeing the wonders of nature: *"Baruch Atah Adonoi, Eloheinu Melech ha-olam, oseh ma'aseh v'reshit.* Blessed art Thou, Lord our God, King of the Universe, who created the universe." The magnificent, natural setting of the camp should provide many occasions for such a blessing, but the counselors told us that, in fact, they never pause with their groups to recite it. They do not incorporate the rabbi's teaching into their own work with the children because they do not see Jewish education as their job.

Centralizing Jewish education in the hands of specialists may be a logical choice in places where counselors lack Judaic knowledge or are otherwise unprepared to take on any part of the educational mission. Bunk counselors are on the front lines of how a camp socializes its children. Unless these counselors have an adequate level of comfort and facility with Jewish content, full decentralization is impossible. One camp hired an educator to design programs and curricula to be implemented by counselors and activity specialists. The educator quickly discovered that the counselors' own Jewish learning was extremely limited. By necessity, she found herself assuming more and more of the direct teaching function at camp. By the time we arrived, the educator was widely seen, by both campers and counselors, as *"the* Jewish presence at camp."

Centralization represents dysfunction in places where the camp is at odds over its Jewish identity. At many of the camps, there were intense disagreements among the leadership about "how Jewish" the camp should be. At one such camp, we could sense the frustration of the rabbis and educators and the hostility of the staff. Senior staff made statements like, "If there's going to be any kind of Jewish content, we'll look to the rabbis and educators to put it wherever it fits in our schedule." When counselors cannot or will not assume part of the responsibility for education, Jewish learning remains confined to whatever box is allocated to the educator.

Decentralization

Decentralization, which pushes Jewish education down into the bunks, is most likely to be feasible in movement camps. In these settings, the counselors typically grew up in the movement and take on their staff positions with a high level of Judaic preparedness. Even here, however, our observation is that continuing education for counselors is necessary. One religious camp, for example, has designed parallel education for counselors and campers. In their *limud* session, counselors study the same curriculum as the campers, albeit at a more adult level. The idea is to enable counselors to talk about, answer questions about, and make references to the formal Jewish educational curriculum at other times of the day.

Even if counselors have sophisticated Judaic knowledge, they may not as yet be expert teachers. Decentralization also requires teacher-friendly materials and a supportive environment. We found examples of such support at a Zionist camp where the counselors work from an extensive curriculum. Organized into a large loose-leaf binder, the curriculum is divided into themes for each age group and provides a variety of options for informal activities related to each theme. The counselors are in partnership with the curriculum writers. Included in the loose-leaf notebook are forms for counselors to complete after each activity, explaining what they did and how it worked. In this way, staff are encouraged to use or depart from the curriculum while contributing to its further development. This process of reviewing activities also makes staff accountable for the daily Jewish/ Zionist education they do with their unit. The curriculum, which appears to be centralized and expert-driven, is enacted in a decentralized manner. Its implementation is in the hands of individual bunk counselors working with their unit heads.

FORMAL AND INFORMAL JEWISH EDUCATION

Formal educational styles are generally associated with schools, informal styles with camps, youth groups, Israel trips and other such settings. It is also the case that any activity— regardless of setting—might be classified as formal, informal, or both depending on how it is carried out. It has been suggested that a key distinction between the two styles resides in the compulsory nature of formal education and the voluntary nature of informal education (Chazan 1991; Shabi and El Ansari 2001). Children are "required" to attend religious school and to prepare for their *b'nei mitzvah* and, for many families, an analogy to castor oil may be understandable. In contrast, with the exception of the few who do not adapt well to camp, most children go off to camp eagerly and willingly and they resist leaving at the end of the summer. The voluntary nature of camp creates an open and relaxed attitude toward education, an attitude not readily translatable to a school setting. This distinction, however, refers to the setting and not to the specific activities that occur within that setting.

Formal and informal education are probably best distinguished by their goals as well as their design. According to Michael Zeldin (1989), formal education has the goal of conveying particular knowledge and skills, and the curriculum, therefore, is written with specific learning objectives. Informal education, in contrast, is based on the notion of "emergent outcomes." Its purpose is to provide rich experiences and then to develop learning out of the participants' responses to those experiences. In Bernard Reisman's view (1990, 1993), the distinction is in the design of activities. Formal education is relatively teacher-centered and content-oriented while informal education is learner-centered and process-oriented (see table 4.1). Based on these distinctions, all of the camps we visited showed evidence of both formal and informal Jewish education.

Formal Jewish Education

Formal Jewish education essentially transports the model of Jewish education found in religious school to the camp setting. Hebrew, text, and Torah are studied with a seriousness of purpose, although learning often takes place under a tree or by the lake instead of in a classroom. For example, the educational program at one of the southern camps we visited

Table 4.1. Aspects of Formal and Informal Education

Educational Variables	Formal	Informal
Educational goals	Students master a prescribed, fixed curriculum in a set period of time.	Participants have a meaningful personal experience that involves fun, socializing, and learning.
View of authority	The teacher is the authority and has power. The teacher is responsible for the content and style of class and for student behavior.	The leader/counselor/teacher empowers group members to learn and to assume responsibility for the group. The leader is a role model and resource.
Normative style of teacher or leader	The teacher is a master of the subject matter. He or she is a good communicator, delivers frontal lectures, is directive.	The leader is a master of process and content. He or she uses creative methods, facilitates interactive group discussion, is non-directive.

Note: Based on B. Reisman. 1990. *Informal Jewish Education in North America.* Report to the Commission on Jewish Education in North America, Cleveland: Mandel Associated Foundations and Jewish Education Service of North America; and B. Reisman. 1993. *Adult Education Trips to Israel: A Transforming Experience.* Jerusalem: Melitz Center for Jewish-Zionist Education.

entails daily classes run by the director of the program, a credentialed teacher. Knowledgeable and dedicated, she runs the entire program herself except for the occasional involvement of visiting rabbis. The curriculum she has developed is extensive, detailed, formal, and frontal. She believes that this is the correct approach because, for many children, one month at camp is their primary opportunity for religious education. From this perspective, not a minute can be wasted.

The *Shabbat* study program at a West Coast denominational camp involves dozens of single-sex group meetings on Saturday afternoon. Each bunk meets for forty-five minutes with a rabbi or senior staff person who is assigned to the group for the entire camp session. The hillside is literally dotted with these groups. The week we visited, the focus was name-calling and lies. We joined a group of twelve- to thirteen-year-old girls and their counselors who were discussing whether they would tell a friend their honest opinion of her way of dressing or whether they would reveal to a shopkeeper the name of a friend who had been caught shoplifting. The discussion, on the part of both campers and staff, was open and frank. According to the education director, the use of senior staff in this way enables the campers to see authority figures in a variety of roles. It also makes clear that everyone is part of the learning process and it advances the idea that anyone can be a Jewish educator in the community.

At a Zionist camp, we observed a less structured, but still formal educational activity. We sat in on a Hebrew *chug,* comprised of eight campers who had chosen conversational Hebrew as an elective. The campers met with two counselors at a picnic table under a shady tree near the dining hall. The class began with a review of the previous day's lesson on introducing oneself in Hebrew. In the next half hour, the group played a counting game in Hebrew, learned casual greetings like *"Mah nishmah?"* ("What's up?"), and planned a skit for presenting the next day's Hebrew Word of the Day to the whole camp.

As we found in our census, most of the camps—including non-Orthodox private camps—offer *bar/bat mitzvah* tutoring. The need to keep twelve-year-olds from forgetting their lessons overrides the intent of camps to be a break from usual studies. At one such camp, about fifty campers signed up for private lessons, which they received a few times a week during rest hour or free period. At this particular camp, families pay extra for this service, which, to us as observers, looked much like a Hebrew class back home. At other camps, tutoring was offered by the camp rabbi on an individual basis, and was free to all who wanted to participate.

What can be accomplished in terms of formal Jewish education depends on the culture of the camp and on campers' expectations. At a camp that is trying to strengthen its Jewish identity, we found a rejection of formal *limud* by both campers and staff. According to the program director, "Kids hate when you take a part of their day out for Jewish education—it reminds them of school." At a teen leadership camp, in contrast, we were told, "if it weren't for the kids, this place would be just buildings and grounds. They push themselves and they push the faculty" to learn more. Rabbis and educators at this camp reported reaching new heights in their teaching during the summer because their campers are so eager and demanding.

Informal Jewish Education

Direct experience, as noted earlier, can form especially strong attitudes that will endure over time. The philosophy of informal Jewish education similarly maintains that meaningful learning results from direct, personal connection to the subject matter (Dewey 1964; Reisman 1978). Informal education usually takes place in a small group that forms a supportive learning community.

At a Zionist movement camp, we observed an activity that embodies the core qualities of informal, experiential education. The seventh grade campers were divided into four groups, each identified with one of Israel's top soccer teams: Maccabi Haifa, Maccabi Tel Aviv, Beitar, and Ha'Poel. The campers put on tee-shirts in their team's color and they learned their team's special cheer. Then they converged in the dining hall where, instead of a live soccer game, they cheered on their counselors who competed with one another on a foosball table. Before the match, a counselor explained the roots of Israeli soccer and the political view represented by each team. During the match, campers were given cups of sunflower seeds to eat and were told to throw the shells on the floor. By the end of the match, the floor was covered with sunflower seeds, just as in a stadium in Israel.

Informal activities such as this Israeli soccer simulation are experiential, sensory, and group-based. When done well, they are also interesting, involving, and fun. The informal learning may be explicitly expressed or implicitly absorbed through the experience itself. We saw ten-year-olds baking *challah* for *Shabbat*—a highly tactile, olfactory, and gustatory experience. They learned about the tradition of removing a piece of dough from the loaf, and they recited the blessing for taking *challah*. We saw twelve-year-olds engage in a lively group competition in which points, to be redeemed for candy, were earned through games that tested knowledge of Hebrew words, Jewish holidays, Jewish practice . . . and their counselors' lives. The amount of candy distributed to the participants was staggering. We went to a *shofar*-making workshop that began with a brief, rabbi-led discussion about the *shofar* (ram's horn) and its use in "waking us up to a new year, and all the opportunities that the new year will offer us." Then we sanded the *shofrot,* learned to blow them, varnished them, and hung them out to dry.

CURRICULUM

Camps are traditional institutions that are loath to change anything they do. Even minor changes in ritual, names, or schedule can provoke strong resistance. At the same time, camps are characterized by a great deal of experimentation, particularly with regard to their Jewish educational mission. Camps, it emerges, are ideal pilot sites for trying new types of programming. A single program can be run multiple times, with a large number of children of varied ages and backgrounds, over a single season. It is a rare opportunity to test out materials and get feedback, then redesign and rerun the program. As Rabbi Daniel Freelander, executive vice-president of the Union of American Hebrew Congregations, reflected, "We could stay up until 2 A.M. writing a song, and then try it out the next day. If it didn't work, we could throw it away and try again" (cited in Fax 1994, p. 52).

Where formal curricula exist, most commonly in the movement camps, they are usually organized by age group, with each group covering a different theme over the course of the session. Table 4.2 displays two of the most developed curricula we saw in action.

Some camps with less extensive intentional Jewish education have a camp-wide theme. One camp develops programs around a single theme in each of its two-week sessions: miracles, heroes, the Jewish-American experience, and Jewish customs. Each week, another camp presents two *midot* (e.g., acting friendly, forgiving others, seeing the other side, being a good winner or loser). The traits thread their way through the week: After *Havdalah,* staff put on a skit about the traits; during the week, large banners promoting them hang in the dining hall; at lunch, campers read handouts with a story or a reminder about them. Finally, after lunch on *Shabbat,* campers who have exhibited the trait during the week are recognized with "Honorable *Mensch*-en Awards," and their names are listed in the annual camp yearbook.

With few exceptions, the camps also have an Israel component in their programming. Israel education is found in special events such as *Yom Yisrael,* in study sessions devoted to Zionism or contemporary issues in Israel, and in Israeli dance classes and singing. As well, a few of the camps had links to Israel trips. Thus, for example, UAHC camps had made participation in the movement's NFTY Israel experience program an expectation

Table 4.2. Examples of Camp Curricula

Grade	Conservative	Zionist
4	Prayer and God (preparation for prayer at camp)	Steps (introduction to Judaism and camping)
5–6	Heroes (history presented through characters)	Israeli culture Jewish calendar and lifecycle events
7	Peace (text-based studies that move from peace in myself to peace in my family, in my community, and in the world)	Jewish identity
8	Ethical decision-making and choices (focused on adolescent issues of drugs, alcohol, sex, body piercing, tattoos, etc.)	Israel—Dream to Reality (first session focused on pre-1948 and second session on 1948–present)
9	Electives (including topics such as the Holocaust, Jewish newspaper, contemporary Israel, *Ecclesiastes*, prayer, lifecycle)	History of Zionism
10		Jewish ethics, morals, and values

for campers between tenth and eleventh grade.[3] A summer trip to Israel was the normal route for those who planned to return to camp the following summer as counselors-in-training. An Israel experience, thus, became part of a camper's "career." Other camps preceded or followed a trip to Israel with a period of residence at the camp. Many of these links to Israel, however, were broken when outbreaks of violence in the Middle East in the summers of 2001 and 2002 caused some sponsors to cancel trips, either out of their own safety concerns or parents' unwillingness to send their teenagers. If security issues persist and participation in trips dwindles, camps will face increasing needs to provide Israel education at camp that matches the power of a visit to the land of Israel.

ELEMENTS OF SUCCESS

Education at camp works partly because of the features that distinguish it from religious school back home. As the educator at a religious camp explained, the approach is hands-on, there are no tests, and the stakes are low. The campers have a different kind of relationship with their counselors than they do with their teachers at school because they hang out with them and interact with them throughout the day. They sit with counselors at mealtime, play basketball with them, pray with them at services, and are tucked in by them at bedtime. Intimate contact and shared activities can profoundly affect the quality of the camper-counselor relationship and its impact on the camper. In addition, the campers see that the counselors themselves go to class. They understand that students and teachers together are part of a learning community at camp, whereas at home they often receive the implicit message that classes are an imposition of the adult world designated solely for children. Moreover, camps make an effort to design Jewish education that has direct relevance to the lives of the campers. Unburdened by the necessity to teach particular content—in preparation for *b'nei mitzvah* or graduation from school—camps are able to deal with material that may otherwise receive short shrift in the educational curriculum.

SOCIALIZATION PROCESSES AT CAMP

Socialization, as described earlier, is a broader process than education. In addition to the acquisition of knowledge, skills, and values, it entails a shift in one's social identity. Socialization is rooted in interpersonal interactions, for it is through relationships with others that the learner comes to identify with the group. Through interactions with counselors and peers, children at camp learn what it means to be a member of a Jewish community. The processes we cited—identification, internalization, and imitation—require that the "teacher" be attractive, credible, and trustworthy. During our participant-observation study, we repeatedly saw these processes in action.

Teachable Moments

Teachable moments are serendipitous moments during the camp day when a child is suddenly but briefly open to learning. Such moments can be encouraged, but unlike formal and informal educational activities, they cannot be planned. Staff training at one of the movement camps emphasizes that every interaction with a child has a potential Jewish educational impact. "We tell the counselors that if a kid has an epiphany about God while brushing his teeth, they need to be alert to that." The point is that when the moment comes, the person to whom the child will turn is his or her counselor, an adult that the child feels he or she can trust. One morning at a movement camp, after a group discussion on the meaning and purpose of the *mezuzah,* the campers hung one on the door of the community hall and they said the blessing. Everyone then rushed off to breakfast, but one boy stayed behind. Something the counselor had said about the way the *mezuzah* is hung differed from what he had learned from his mother and he was curious. The counselor and boy walked off together toward the dining hall, deep in conversation.

Unanticipated events may occur that create teachable moments for both campers and staff. When her father died unexpectedly, Sarah left camp. Her eighteen-year-old counselor, Jo, had to handle the reactions of Sarah's bunkmates. Jo had to shepherd the girls through a week of coping with loss—not only of Sarah's father (a single parent who had a larger-than-life quality for many of the girls), but of their friend who had left camp. And she also had to respond to the girls as they revealed their concerns about how best to support Sarah. Jo consulted with the camp director and it was decided that the bunk would go, as a group, to see Sarah during the *shiva* (mourning) week.

To prepare the girls for the visit, she turned to other staff members who had been through losses. These staffers met with the girls, spoke about their own experiences, and talked about the role of the community in supporting the mourner. It just so happened that the following week it was Jo's turn to present the *d'var Torah* at services. In her comments on that *Shabbat,* she told how she had to learn quickly about Jewish mourning practices and appropriate communal responses. She reported that she had spent many hours in the camp library reading each day as she encountered new aspects of this challenge. In this example, we see multifaceted teaching and learning occurring as campers and staff struggle with a life event. We see an environment that supports such learning and has the resources and flexibility that allow people to grab the moment. And we see campers who were ready to learn and, equally important, staff who were ready to teach.

Role Modeling

As we described in chapter 1, some psychological theorists argue that imitation is the most important source of social learning. In this regard, the power of the counselor as role model should not be underestimated. The importance of role modeling is emphasized in staff training. A staff manual at a denominational camp, for example, refers to the unit head as "the ultimate role model." Unit heads are instructed as follows: *"Shacharit* (morning prayers) is one of the rare visible times during the day when you are the leader of the whole *edah* (unit) and everyone is looking to you for leadership. You should be loud, energetic, happy, and positive. This attitude will carry over to your counselors and campers. You should also make sure that you are at *t'fillot* on time, every day."

A male counselor at another ritually observant camp told us that he saw his role during *t'fillot* as modeling proper prayer behavior. He said that a number of ten- to twelve-year-old boys had recently begun to imitate the counselors' practices of wearing *t'fillin* (phylacteries), waving *tzitzit* (knotted strands on the corner of a prayer shawl), *shokling* (swaying during prayer), and standing for the mourner's *Kaddish*. The counselors model and the campers "try on" the behavior. The counselors of the younger children said that their campers do not come to them to discuss rituals or issues of Jewish identity, but they do sidle up to them during *t'fillot* and copy their movements. The counselors see this as the way the children express their questions—looking to the counselors to model appropriate behavior.

Counselors who are admired can communicate a great deal simply by showing campers that they take Judaism seriously. One counselor had a group of campers who did not appreciate services and had difficulty behaving properly during them. She decided to talk to the campers about the problem. "Services can be kind of long and boring," she told them, "and you might not understand them. But you have to respect them. If you're bored, you're bored. Just sit there and read the prayer book. It's all very simple; it's all written out. Services are not a time for being social. You might not understand them, but you have to respect them because some people take them seriously." "Who takes it seriously?" one of the girls challenged her. "*I* take it seriously," the counselor replied.

Given the power of role models to influence behavior, it is also the case that counselors and senior staff can model inappropriate or disrespectful behaviors. At Friday night services at one movement camp, many of the campers were restless. They talked and played with friends and were obviously distracted and unengaged in prayer. The senior staff, however, were equally unengaged. One was circling a nearby field in a golf cart and others were carrying on their own conversations. The unruly campers were, in fact, merely imitating the behavior of the adult models. Throughout our study, we found that camper and staff behavior, whether positive or negative, was almost always in synchrony—with counselors providing the model and campers following suit.

Trying on Behaviors
Modeling influences behavior only if the learner imitates the model. The environment at camp that supports experimentation and learning thus plays a key role in socialization. Camps, at their best, establish an environment where campers and staff can explore their Judaism, ask questions, and try on new practices and behaviors. Camp as camp supports and encourages campers to try out a new sport or audition for a play. Camp as a Jewish experience supports campers in trying out *t'fillin,* leading services, or reading Torah. We saw an Israeli staff member alone on a porch, *davening,* and learned that she had never prayed before she came to camp. We saw a camper teaching a counselor to read Torah for her first time.[4] One morning we heard campers who had just learned to lay *t'fillin* recite the morning prayers. A counselor told us, "I really like the curiosity in the kids, the way they pull me over quietly during *davening.* I had an eleven year old, so curious that he wants to put on my *t'fillin.* And he came up to me yesterday, begging me, just wanting the experience, wanting to be able to feel what it's like."

MISSED OPPORTUNITIES
Although much of the Jewish educational programming at summer camps appears successful, the full potential of camps to educate has hardly been realized. To be sure, our field observations are replete with positive examples of both formal and informal education, but they also include failed activities and poor teaching. Consistent with other research, we noted that

girls seem more engaged than boys (Kadushin, Kelner, and Saxe 2000); there are moments of joy in learning but also moments of boredom; there are those who attend as expected and required and those who skip class; there are activities that run well and others that are stopped due to disruptive behavior and lack of interest. Overall, we witnessed two types of missed opportunities at camp: failure to create opportunities for Jewish learning and failure to capitalize on such opportunities.

Failure to Create the Opportunity

At one camp, the arts-and-crafts center has materials that could be used to make Judaica, but the specialist in charge prepares no Jewish arts-and-crafts projects. The drama specialist, trained specifically to work in a Jewish setting, chooses no plays with Jewish themes. Another camp's final musical production of the season is *The Sound of Music*. We observe the troupe rehearsing the scene in which Maria is told to leave the convent. We see Jewish girls playing nuns, and counselors trying to block out the scene, deciding where the lead should bow to the Mother Superior, where she should kiss her ring, and so on. When we ask the director about the choice of plays, she replies that, as far as she knows, there are no plays with Jewish themes that have casts large enough for a camp production. In our role as outside observers, we simply nod. We are aware of the failure to choose a Jewish play and of the failure to use effectively the play that was chosen. The director missed an opportunity to teach about Judaism or about views of other faith traditions.

Camps often leave it up to the specialists to decide what they will do, including whether or not their area will have Jewish content. We asked the arts-and-crafts specialists at one camp how they choose their projects. They said that they plan activities to suit the number of hours they have with a group, to merit the amount of money parents pay, and to avoid duplication of projects done in the past. Given these criteria, it is not surprising that the arts-and-crafts shed, aside from "Shalom" signs painted in English, gives little evidence of being in a Jewish camp.

At another camp, where Judaica is found around the arts-and-crafts shed, the specialist told us that he had found some books at camp with ideas for Jewish crafts. He admitted that, had he not come across the books, it would not have occurred to him to add Jewish content to the arts-and-crafts program. The environmental education counselor at this camp told a different story. In preparing her program, she chose not to incorporate Judaism because she "really doesn't know anything about it." If she were more comfortable with her Jewish knowledge, she said, she would tie Judaism into the environmental program.

Failure to Capitalize on Opportunity

We also noted failure to make good use of Jewish learning opportunities. For example, the *teva* program at a denominational movement camp wanted to involve campers in thinking about recycling paper and saving trees. The design called for campers to cycle through four different activities in one hour. Staff thus found themselves with fifteen minutes to engage campers in the following problem: "The national movement has approved the recycling of old *siddurim* (prayer books) and the camp has more than one hundred such books that they want to get rid of. We are to develop a ritual for disposing of these books." Fifteen minutes quickly passed, leaving no time for the group to reach a conclusion to its discussion.

At an Orthodox private camp, we went with the senior girls to a Friday afternoon *challah*-making workshop. The leader of the workshop explained to us that it was just an activity. It entailed no teaching, just bread baking. At a Jewish community center camp, we stood in line to participate in the ritual washing of hands before the special Friday night meal. Some of the campers in line with us had never washed before and were taking the opportunity to try out this practice. No leader offered an explanation of the ritual or the prayer. When our turn came, we noticed that, next to the beautiful bowl set out for washing, there was a prayer written in Hebrew with transliteration. Unfortunately, it was the blessing for bread and not the one for the washing of hands. A Zionist camp ran an alternative service where counselors taught about *t'fillin*. About twenty campers came and asked questions. However, there were no *t'fillin* at camp for the campers to use. The staff also teaches about *tzitzit* but do not think about giving the boys a chance to try wearing them for a day. In all of these instances, learning opportunities were missed because of flawed program design, inadequate resources, or failure to make use of a teachable moment.

Jewish camping is rife with opportunities to develop original curricula, to explore new ways of integrating Jewish education into everyday camp activities, and to refine the techniques of informal Jewish education. Programming, however, does not stand on its own but depends almost entirely on staff. Whether in leading activities, grasping a teachable moment, modeling Jewish values and behavior, or supporting children as they try on new behaviors, it is the staff members' knowledge, ability to relate to the campers, and facilitation and programming skills that are most critical to success. Ultimately, camp's power as a socializing agent resides in its capacity for fun and friendship. Education at camp—in formal and informal educational activities and in everyday interactions—is like candy, and its ultimate success lies within its sweetness.

5

The Fresh Air of Judaism

JEWISH LIFE AT CAMP

The Hebrew word *neshamah* means soul, but it also refers to breath. It connects the divine with the physical in the same way that God breathed life into Adam (Gen. 2.7). Metaphorically, the same connection exists at camp. At the camps we visited, Judaism was "in the air." We found it in everyday ritual practices, in *Shabbat,* and in the symbolism that defines the physical environment of the camp as Jewish space. When Judaism is in the air, as it is at many camps, children take it in as effortlessly as breathing.

Jewish camps—whether they are movement, community, or private camps—negotiate the level of their Jewishness. Some camps abide by traditional views of *halachah* (Jewish law) and offer campers and staff a summer of adherence to *kashrut, Shabbat* observance, and other practices governed by Jewish law. Other camps offer Jewish life that is not governed by *halachah*. Their practice of *kashrut* may be liberal and idiosyncratic and their *Shabbat* observance may incorporate electric guitars unapologetically filling the community hall with music.[1]

Some camps arrived at their "formula" years ago. They are comfortable with the extent to which Jewish customs and education are incorporated into the camp program and their leaders are disinclined to discuss or change it. Several of the camps included in our field study, however, are wrestling over their Jewish identities and practices. In some cases, there are differences between the national movements and local practices or between espoused and actual practices. Some camp leaders openly acknowledge and discuss these discrepancies; others are more reticent. Staff members at one of the nondenominational camps even consider the inconsistencies in the camp's Jewish practices a strength of the camp, a sign that it is not "getting carried away" with a particular Jewish viewpoint. In other cases, camps are in transition, intentionally creating new Jewish identities and transforming their Jewish practices. The wrestling here is more dynamic, more apparent to the outside observer.

At all of the camps, the director, sometimes with other senior staff, sets the tone. In addition to performing a myriad of duties related to the camp's health, safety, and financial viability, the director acts as a religious authority. Although influenced by lay boards and other interested parties, decisions about prayer, dietary laws, and the centrality (or not) of Jewish education are made by the director on site. Even when following mandates from the national movement, the director governs implementation.

EVERYDAY PRACTICES

We studied in detail four everyday practices at camp: prayer, song, *kashrut,* and mealtime blessings. These practices, found at each of the camps we visited, encompass a range of distinctly Jewish religious behaviors.

T'fillot

At camps with daily *t'fillot* (whether a service in the chapel or morning prayers said in the dining hall), prayer becomes a natural part of the campers' everyday life. Children are socialized into prayer at camp with consistency and repetition. Through repetition, prayers are learned and camp prayer tradition formed. Even as outsiders, we quickly had melodies and prayer experiences irresistibly floating through our heads. In the same way, campers arriving at camp unable to read Hebrew or *daven,* readily learn Jewish rituals and the words and melodies to dozens of prayers and Hebrew songs.

Because camps are tradition-bound institutions with deeply ingrained norms, it is difficult to change their rituals and worship services. Often, the camp's particular form of worship services has evolved over many years. Each year, it is carried on by returning campers who, in turn, socialize the next generation of campers. In some settings, such transmission of camp tradition fosters religious engagement, but in other settings, where services have been perfunctory, it can obstruct efforts to increase the intensity of the Jewish experience.

Several markers of the quality of *t'fillot* at camp were easily discerned: the involvement of campers as prayer leaders, the level of *kavanah* (concentration, devotion) during prayer, the presence of a Torah scroll, and the extent to which services replicate a standard Jewish service or create a sui generis prayer experience.

Who leads services? Each camp has its own method of conducting services. We attended daily and *Shabbat* services led by the camp director, the Jewish educator, counselors, or campers. Although we expected camper-led services to be the most involving for the children, overall, we found that the level of participation during services is unrelated to who conducts them. At a private camp where campers lead services for their own age group, the Jewish educator complained that it was difficult to find enough campers who had the experience, ability, and willingness to lead services. The younger campers had the motivation, but not the knowledge. The older campers had the knowledge but lacked the motivation. To overcome this problem, the senior boys coordinator had resorted to incentives, offering the boys who would lead services the privilege of going first through the buffet line at the Friday evening meal. In contrast, at a camp where services are designed, led, and strictly controlled by the educator, campers formed a long line during "open mike" time, eager to read a poem or thought piece they had found in a book or had written themselves. It took thirty minutes to get through the line.

Many camps have a mixed model of leadership in which the rabbi and/ or educator work assiduously to prepare campers to lead services. Their coaching includes helping campers learn to chant Torah, to write original prayers, and to prepare a camp version of a *d'var Torah*. The goal is to find ways to engage campers during services. Given this goal, a critical role at most camps is that of the song leader who leads *shirim* (songs, songfest), often with the help of older campers and counselors-in-training.

Is there kavanah? "Some kids will ask me questions, and some are very interested, and some would rather sleep through Saturday morning services," a counselor told us. This latter attitude was most prevalent at camps whose Jewish mission was in transition and at camps where the leadership was ambivalent about the way the camp should express its Judaism. At these camps, the campers often participated in services unenthusiastically or with obvious resistance. We attended a Monday teen *Shacharit* service (morning prayers) at a movement camp. Some of the campers arrived in pajamas, clearly sleepy. Most participated in a perfunctory manner, sitting through the *Amidah* and barely opening the prayer book. We attended *Kabbalat Shabbat* (a prayer service marking the start of *Shabbat*) at a community camp where a brief service was poorly printed on paper sheets that should have been recycled long ago. No *kipot* (skullcaps) were available and the few participants wearing head coverings were counselors (not campers, not senior staff). During the service, some of the campers were attentive and eagerly participated, but many were unruly, talking and disrupting those around them. At one point, the service had to be stopped to restore order. At *Shabbat* morning services at other camps, we observed various signs of disinterest: At one service, few children recited the *Sh'ma* or joined in with other prayers or songs. At another, the song leaders tried unsuccessfully to engage the campers in singing *"Hinei Ma Tov."* At a third, we primarily heard the counselors' voices in prayers, and it seemed that most of the time the campers were just sitting there. Yet, when the Torah was carried through the community, the younger campers were suddenly animated, eager to touch it.

We also attended services, most notably *Kabbalat Shabbat* and *Havdalah,* where the power of prayer and song was palpable, and the singing elevated and transformed the gathering. We were in the bunks for a bedtime ritual filled with tenderness and spirituality: The sixth-grade girls had gotten into bed, heard a story, and were settled in for the night. The lights were turned out and the whole group sang the *Sh'ma* and the *Ve'ahavta.* Then the counselors made the rounds to all the girls and kissed them goodnight. It was a beautiful end to the camp day. In these instances, youth, *ruach,* and the camp setting coalesced to create a worship experience that reverberated in our own minds even after we had left the camp.

What are the counselors doing? Adult role models set the tone for worship at camp. They were thus implicated in almost every instance of disinterest in or disrespect for prayer. When camp leaders and counselors made obvious their own lack of involvement, campers responded with restlessness rather than *kavanah*. Counselors, who are to be guides and role models during services, sometimes fulfilled that role and sometimes did not.

Although we saw many examples of positive staff influence, staff behavior was most noticeable when it distracted. For example, during Friday night services, some of the counselors sat in rows with the campers, while others sat in the back of the chapel and talked throughout the service. The unit heads stood in back, and the director walked around taking pictures (presumably for the camp website). During *Shabbat* morning services, Israeli staff were disrespectful and the prayer leader stopped the service to reprimand them in Hebrew. A counselor sat in the back of the amphitheater reading her mail throughout the service. Other counselors acted as patrols, keeping the children in line by "bopping" offenders on the head. Many staff and some specialists sat on the periphery, outside the chapel. Such disengagement or disrespect is not confined to a single camp. In fact, each of these behaviors was seen at a different camp.

Where is the Torah? The Torah scroll is the most cherished of Jewish religious objects and Torah study is an important focus of *Shabbat* observance. Most, but not all, of the camps in our study had at least one Torah scroll. We saw scrolls that were kept in a homemade ark, an ark inherited from a synagogue, or an ark built for the camp chapel. In some of these camps, the Torah is not used; in others it is read only once a session on *Shabbat;* in still others it is regularly taken out of the ark at services but the actual reading is done from a sheet of paper or prayer book, not from the scroll. Interviews with camp directors and educators revealed the reasons why the Torah remains in the ark. Camps do not read from the Torah regularly in some cases because they do not have enough people at camp who can do the reading and, in other cases, because they fear that the Torah service will not sustain the interest of campers. In particular, there is a concern that the service will remind campers of the home synagogues that they do not like to attend.

In contrast, at the insistence of a visiting rabbi, one camp now uses the Torah scroll during *Shabbat* services. Torah reading was introduced here through a gradual process. At first, the rabbi merely brought the Torah scroll with him when he came to camp each weekend. Later, he used it as a "ritual object." The process culminated the summer of our study. That year, several staff members had a *b'nei mitzvah* celebration at camp and publicly read Torah for the first time.

Would the services be recognizable in a congregation back home? Some of the Jewish camps we studied intentionally use liturgy common among congregations in their movement or among congregations in their campers' home communities. They want to ensure that what campers learn during the summer will be applicable back home. Liturgy aside, worship services are molded to suit the camp environment and the culture of the particular camp. Thus, at *Shabbat* morning services at a community camp, the educator conducts an interactive *d'rash* (homily) on the *parashah,* asking campers questions about the sequence of events in the later books of the Torah and the roles played by Moses and Joshua after Sinai. In a comfortable and engaging way, she invites campers to fill in details of the events and she rewards answers by throwing candy to respondents. At several other camps, Saturday morning services include a dramatic presentation rather than the study of Torah text per se. A skit, developed from a brief synopsis of the weekly *parashah,* is performed by one of the bunks and a discussion follows.

At some camps, campers and staff are encouraged to create and recite original prayers during services. We listened as an eleven-year-old girl sang a song she had written about friendship—particularly moving for the end of a camp session when new and old friends would be saying goodbye. We watched as a counselor sang a beautiful song at the end of the *Shabbat* morning service and members of the congregation closed their eyes and held hands. One camp took the opportunity to create an entirely original prayer book when the need arose to replace the old ones that it had inherited from a congregation years ago. The program director took on the challenge of translating the essence of the prayers into child-friendly language. She created a layout with spaces next to the prayers for artwork. Weekly Judaica classes became prayer through art as the campers were guided in drawing about their feelings and interpretations of the liturgy. These drawings were then inserted in the books opposite the Hebrew prayers. By the end of the summer, each prayer book was fully illustrated by the campers.

Sometimes the creative energy at camp services confounds the sacred and the profane. At *Kabbalat Shabbat* services at a movement camp, we saw members of the dance group perform to *"Bo'i Kalah"* by the popular Israeli singer/songwriter Achinoam Nini. Their dance was well-choreographed, involving a jazzy quality with many of the hip-thrusting and sexy moves modeled earlier by their Israeli dance instructor. The highlight of the service at another movement camp is the melody chosen for *"Adon Olam,"* a prayer about the eternal kingship of God. Options ranged from the tune of "Yellow Submarine" (a Beatles' song), the "William Tell Overture" (of Lone Ranger fame), or "Barbie Girl"(an up-beat, rhythmic, sexy rendition complete with "uh-huh, uh-huhs").

Original prayers, skits, dance, music, and artwork—often derived directly from the prevailing youth culture—make services at camp a creative, involving, youth-centric event that often clashes with synagogue services back home. As Fox (1997) notes, the warm and informal tone of worship at camp can cause re-entry problems for campers at the end of summer. Campers may find it difficult to return to a synagogue service that seems stilted, complacent, and formal compared to their camp's service. Although the unbridled originality and youth energy that characterize camp services may be out of place back home, they make sense in the camp setting and create a prayer experience that can be both deeply Jewish and uniquely camp.

At the same time, campers at the liberal camps develop curious ritual practices and idiosyncratic customs. According to camp faculty, who are fascinated by the process, one camper invents a meaningless prayer practice that sweeps through the camp and becomes standard practice. At one camp, for example, all of the campers rise up on their toes when they say the names of the patriarchs and matriarchs during prayers. This phenomenon is less likely to occur at traditional camps where we often saw great attention paid to correct prayer behavior. Campers are told not to rush to kiss the Torah as it is carried about the hall but to wait until it comes to them, *lichvod ha'Torah* (in respect for the Torah). They are instructed to place their prayer books only front side up in the crates at the end of services, *lichvod ha'siddur* (in respect for the prayer book).

Just as a tour of the congregations in any community would produce an array of prayer experiences that differ by congregation, denomination, and spiritual leadership, so too does the Jewish camping world serve as a setting for a great range of experiences. Most are positive, and deepen participants' feelings toward Judaism. A few, as described above, are uninspired or negative, and probably do little to motivate continued participation in Jewish worship.

Shirim

"Shiru l'Adonai Shir Hadash"—"Sing a new song unto the Lord." So reads the quotation engraved on the outside of the community hall. The inscription is most appropriate. Song is everywhere and the role of song at camp cannot be overstated. Song is heard in the dining room at mealtime, at *t'fillot*, at camp meetings, in the bunks, at activities. Some camps include song sessions as a regular camp activity, scheduled along with swimming and arts and crafts. These sessions are generally used to teach new songs. Then there are sessions—planned and spontaneous—in which the camp breaks out into song.

Song is used to bring order to chaos in the dining hall, to build community, and to create spiritual moments. It brings groups together, it energizes, it creates mood. The song leaders are heroes at camp. Particular songs or melodies are part and parcel of the camp culture and tradition. Sharing those tunes unites members of the camp community—like a secret society—both at camp and back home. "At school during the year," one counselor told us, "a word will come up and there will always be a song from camp that connects and all the camp people will break out in song. People who come from the Israel program will start dancing to it . . ." Several camps have recently produced compact discs with songs from camp so that memories can be evoked throughout the year.

At our first Friday night at a camp, songbooks and play lists were handed out after Friday night dinner. The music director stood at an electronic keyboard with a headset mike. One, two, three—she kicked off the *Shabbat zemirot* (songs celebrating the Sabbath). We were participant observers and did not know exactly what to expect—a half hour? an hour? Amazingly, the singing continued for two hours, all in Hebrew. Everyone knew the lyrics and the special hand motions and movements for each song. Everyone knew when to get up and dance. The music covered every genre from folk to spiritual to upbeat pop. The campers, with arms around each other, were transfixed by the music. Their voices were beautiful. The camp sang into the night.

Song succeeds where other activities may fail. We were at camps where the *davening* was lackluster but the hours-long *Shabbat* song session was engaged with great enthusiasm. Led by the song leaders, campers would sing a wide range of Jewish songs that involved hand movements, stomping, parading, tango sequences, and other high-spirited, noisy activity. The vibrancy of these song sessions greatly contrasted with the more subdued prayer services.

Although song is not the province of any one denomination, the Reform movement deserves much credit for the work it has done to educate and train song leaders. The guitar is the hallmark of Reform song leaders. One day at Kutz Camp (the Reform movement's leadership camp) we walked through the main lodge past a row of forty-eight guitar cases learning against a wall. These guitars represent four dozen song leaders in training. At Kutz's teen leadership camp, every camper participates in two song sessions every day.

Kashrut

Directors set the standard for *kashrut* at their camps based on a combination of factors: personal beliefs, the practical issues involved in serving a particular camper population, and directives from owners, national parent organizations, and lay boards. For example, a Reform camp that identifies its menu as "kosher style" has its own list of permissible and non-permissible foods: It does not serve pork products, but it does serve spaghetti with meat sauce and grated cheese. It has kosher hotdogs at the camp barbeque, an option of kosher chicken on *Shabbat,* as well as a vegetarian option at every meal. In contrast, the kitchen at a pluralistic camp is under Orthodox supervision. The summer of our study, it had a *mashgiach* (supervisor) on site two days a week. It was intending to have a full-time *mashgiach* the following season so that it could hold to the highest standard of *kashrut* and, thereby, not exclude any camper.

The private camps we studied have kosher kitchens and purchase all their food only from approved lists. Beyond this basic similarity, their standards vary considerably. One has a full-time *mashgiach* and holds to a strict level of *kashrut* under the supervision of a local Orthodox rabbi. Another has two sets of dishes but only one dishwasher. At one camp, counselors take away any *treif* (non-kosher food) that the campers receive from home or bring back from field trips. At another, the campers can get candy snacks made with milk almost immediately after a meat meal. They can have meat and cheese sandwiches on overnight outings and can go to McDonald's on field trips. One counselor described *kashrut* at this camp as merely "symbolic." The observance of *kashrut* is, of course, not simply a symbolic act, but affects who, among potential campers and counselors, feels welcome and able to live in the camp community. As a result, most camps establish a standard of *kashrut* that has ramifications for camper and staff recruitment that the camp can accept.

Mealtime and *Birkat Ha'mazon*

Mealtime is an important occasion in camp life. Although the quality of the culinary experience varies from camp to camp, meals everywhere function as valuable community time. They are the occasion for everyone to gather together and to check in with one another. They are a time for announcements, planning, joking, and singing. One camp has skits after lunch that promote upcoming activities. The counselors and campers devote so much time and energy to creating these skits, the director joked, that they are often more polished than the actual programs. At other camps, Israeli counselors teach Hebrew words through brief mealtime skits. In most places, campers sit at meals with their bunks. At one camp, table assignments are rotated so that campers get to know the whole camp community, not just those in their bunk or unit. One camp has *shirim* after every meal, with the whole camp singing Israeli and Hebrew songs. Crowded camps that need to divide campers into separate dining halls or serve meals in shifts miss this regular time of camp community building. It is also missed in those few places where mealtimes are so chaotic and noisy that staff make community announcements only with great difficulty.

In almost all camps, the Jewishness of the setting is reinforced by the singing of *Birkat Ha'mazon*. This blessing, recited at group meals, is an omnipresent marker of Jewish life that assumes a unique quality at each camp. It thus serves as an emblem for everyday Jewish practices at camp, an indicator of campers' and counselors' level of engagement, respect, and spirit. At one camp, for example, campers easily quiet down for the blessing, which is led by a designated bunk. The blessing is sung respect-fully, with multi-part harmony. At another camp, the Jewish educators are like guards patrolling during a highly abbreviated version of the *Birkat Ha'mazon*. At a third camp, *Birkat Ha'mazon* is treated as a fun song. A staff member explained: "We've turned it into a song with clapping and with movements. It's not really treated as if it's a prayer—although it is a prayer and we're saying it for a reason. The kids think of it more as a song, and a way to end the meal with festivity. It's a positive thing." At a fourth, the blessing has become a chant, with campers engaging in lots of pounding, hand motions, funny sounds, and silly, made-up lyrics.

As in all areas of Jewish ritual, counselors play a key role in how *Birkat Ha'mazon* is approached. Where counselors model respect, campers are more likely to show respect as well. The camp, too, has a role to play. At some camps, there were campers who did not seem to know the blessing and there were no *bentchers* readily available or distributed.[2] Even when sheets were distributed, they sometimes contained errors that none of the education staff had bothered to point out or correct.

RELIGIOUS DAYS

Camps have different ways to carve out sacred time. Some reserve it for *Shabbat;* others make room for sacred time every day. Some start *Shabbat* early and savor its every moment; others start late or end early. In all cases, however, the separation of time is complete, intentional, and palpable.

Shabbat

Camp is ideally suited for *Shabbat* observance, and even the most secular Jewish camps in our study make *Shabbat* a special time. In fact, in these settings, *Shabbat* is when Jewish activity is seen most clearly. The days of the week at camp are an indistinguishable flow of time. Campers may not even know what day it is—except for *Shabbat,* the one day of the week that stands out from all the others. At an Orthodox private camp, thoughts of *Shabbat* start as early as Monday. While making announcements to the camp or talking about something unrelated to *Shabbat,* the director will suddenly ask, "Do you know what's coming?" The entire camp responds in unison, *"Shabbes* is coming!"

Everyone—directors, administrators, counselors, campers—tells us that

Shabbat at camp is very special. When we were unable to arrange our site visit to include *Shabbat,* members of the camp community expressed their regrets and were quick to tell us that we were missing "the best" part of camp. Because of their isolation, camps have a unique opportunity to separate *Shabbat* from the rest of the week. They change the everyday schedule for *Shabbat* and suspend regular activities. They have late wake-up on Saturday morning. Flowers are on the tables and special decorations are hung around the dining hall. There is special (and better) food. The pace is different. In many of the camps, there is no traffic in or out of camp on *Shabbat.* The place shuts down and even the most secular are drawn into the beauty of a peaceful day.

One director says the approach of *Shabbat* at camp feels like Friday afternoon in Israel. "Around two o'clock on Friday afternoon," she explains, "everything slows down. It's not intentional. It just happens like that." Preparation for *Shabbat* begins with *nikayon,* a camp clean-up. Each unit is responsible for its bunks and for one area of the camp grounds. Even the maintenance crews, busy with other tasks during the week, are out trimming the lawn outside the cabins. Once the physical environment is cleaned, there is time for personal preparation. The camp emerges at last, all dressed in white, ready to greet the Sabbath.

Each camp has its own *Shabbat* customs and its own special ways of setting the mood and expressing the meaning of the day. These customs are the material of camp memories. At a movement camp, strolling guitarists start from all ends of the camp and the community follows the musicians to the *Mercaz* (central meeting area) for *Kabbalat Shabbat.* A visiting rabbi tells a *Shabbat* story, everyone sings *Shabbat* songs, a group presents a brief dance, and then the community moves into the dining hall. Friday night dinner here is the one meal at which campers can choose where to sit, and it is often a time for siblings to join together. Candle, wine, and *challah* blessings are led by visiting rabbis. There is wine (grape juice) and *challah* on every table. Dinner is followed by an abundantly energetic songfest whose excitement is magnified by electrified guitars and microphones. The first segment is comprised of all up-tempo songs, which are mostly in Hebrew. Everyone stands and uses hand movements to each song. Then, almost suddenly, the entire camp moves to the perimeter of the dining room and joins in a giant friendship circle, arm over arm, swaying to more mellow tunes.

At a second camp, the special ritual is *"sukkat shalom"* (shelter of peace), in which counselors hold a *tallit* (prayer shawl) open over the heads of the campers, creating a connection among the campers under the canopy as well as among the counselors holding it. In many ways, this ritual serves a similar purpose to the tradition of parents' blessing their children on *Shabbat*. At a third camp, the focal ritual is candle lighting. *Kabbalat Shabbat* services at this camp are held in the gym where a long table is set up along the back wall with hundreds of unlit candles. Once the campers are assembled, the girls light the candles and recite the blessing with the assistance of several women volunteers.

At a fourth camp, *Shabbat* is welcomed with a service held in the camp's outdoor sanctuary. The distinction between everyday and *Shabbat* is noteworthy. On Friday night, the campers seem transformed in their grooming, their clothes, and their demeanor. They act like a large family of loving, respectful siblings. Led by the camp's song leaders, *Kabbalat Shabbat* is mostly chanted. We were there only one week after the start of the session but already the campers knew the words of each prayer and acted disappointed when the service concluded. Normally, campers eat in two shifts, but on Friday night they all squeeze into the dining hall for a chicken dinner. Dinner, it turns out, is merely the preparation for an after-dinner songfest—camp songs, Debbie Friedman tunes, and secular music. The night winds up with Israeli folk dancing.

Shabbat is also a special time for staff. Counselors refuse to take *Shabbat* off—even when it is their assigned day—because they do not want to miss a single *Shabbat* at camp. They have their own *oneg* (reception), sometimes at the director's home, with deli meats, fancy pastries, candy, fresh fruit, and motivational words from the director. Everyone comes; the place is packed. Conversation is animated and there is a warm, family feeling.

We saw only a few exceptions to these positive descriptions. At a couple of camps, there was little *Shabbat* enthusiasm, particularly among older campers. At one camp, the leadership regularly uses *Shabbat* as a day off, in effect turning over the camp to the Judaic specialists and junior staff. To our minds, these camps have undermined camping's best tool for Jewish socialization—a memorable *Shabbat* experience.

Tishah B'Av

By happenstance of the calendar, *Tishah B'Av* is the only Jewish holiday that falls during the summer months. A commemoration of the destruction of the Temple in Jerusalem, in its essence it is not the kind of holiday that one would associate with camp. In a setting where mealtime is community time, *Tishah B'Av* is a day of fasting. In a place where the primary value is fun, *Tishah B'Av* is about mourning.

Some camps have reworked the meaning of the holiday to bring it into line with the tone and tenor of camp, to shift the focus toward the positive, vibrant Jewish experience and away from the sad and guilty association of the Jew as victim. One camp treats *Tishah B'Av* as a "day of celebration," a time to look at Jewish history and rejoice at how far the Jewish people have come. Another avoids serious programming on *Tishah B'Av;* instead, it presents "Purim in August"—an excuse for celebration, singing, and dressing up in costumes.

Other places, sometimes with great debate amongst camp leaders, have turned *Tishah B'Av* into a day of Holocaust remembrance. At one such camp, the evening ceremony started with quiet songs like *"Dona Dona"* and "The Sound of Silence." Everyone was dressed in black except the tenth graders, who wore white to symbolize hope. The benches in the chapel were set up in a spiral. While a violin played in the background, readers told the story of a girl whose life was saved during the Holocaust by her violin. Then the whole camp walked in a chain to the beach where they burned a sign, made out of wire and cloth, that read *"Zachor"* (Remember). The campers we spoke with said that the program gave them "sad memories," "a sense of how lucky we are," and "a lot to think about."

Still other camps observe the holiday in its more traditional form. They conduct special educational sessions about the holiday; they refrain from singing, dancing, or cheering; they cancel some of their regular activities. They serve only vegetarian meals that day and/or make a vegetarian option available to everyone in the week preceding the holiday. They offer no afternoon snack and no desserts on the holiday. At one camp, the drama teacher produced a play about *Tishah B'Av.* Even though rehearsals took place during free time, seventy-five campers signed up to be in the play.

Because this has not been a major holiday for American Jewry, camp is often the first time children encounter it. Many use this as an opportunity to "try on" fasting and related observances. Fasting is an option at all the camps we visited. Indeed, at one camp we saw dozens of campers who had chosen to fast sitting together by the lake during mealtime. In order to fast, a camper has to be of a certain age and to have parental permission. As in all matters at camp, health and safety come first.

JUDAISM IN THE ENVIRONMENT

The physical environment is often thought of as a means of "passive Jewish education." The environment is, in fact, a powerful force that shapes behavior and sends out the message that this is a Jewish place. As we entered each camp in our observational study, we were aware of crossing the border from a mostly Gentile world into a Jewish world. Soon after we drove out of Atlanta, heading toward one of the southern camps, the hills began, the foliage changed, and rebel flags appeared as did "little black Sambo" statues on front lawns. After almost two hours, we saw the first sign for the camp. It was a brown and white sign, placed back from the road and nearly covered by trees. It had no Hebrew or logo of any kind, as if not to offend the neighbors. Further along, however, we found the camp road and on it the entrance sign sporting the familiar logo and Hebrew motto. As Jews, we somehow felt we were home.

Symbols abound in the camp environment. At various camps, we observed a large (six-foot or more) Star of David at the main entrance to the camp or on top of a mountain overlooking the camp, Hebrew language and Israeli posters on the walls of dining halls and community halls, the *Aleph Bet* carved on tiles around the swimming pool and inflatable Hebrew letters floating in the pool, camp roads named for sites in Israel, Jewish National Fund posters in the *teva* (nature) cabin showing different environments in Israel, and Israeli music pouring forth from loud speakers in the dining hall.

Sometimes the symbols communicate a mixed message. One camp flies an American flag on the flagpole but no Israeli flag. A second names its bunks after Israeli cities but uses American forms (e.g., Jerusalem instead of Yerushalayim) and spells them with the Roman alphabet. A third has a large *L'Chaim* sign in Hebrew but has misspelled it (with the letter *hay* instead of *chet*). Such omissions and errors were most often noted in camps struggling with their Jewish identities.

Sacred Space

The location designated for worship services is emblematic of each camp's view of worship. At one camp, the amphitheater sanctuary is physically located in the center of the camp. At others, the sacred space is set off in the woods or by the lake, away from the main activity center of the camp. We attended services in a chapel comprised of rows of benches and a hand-carved ark. This space is designated for services and is used for no other purpose; it is held as the camp's sacred space. Worship services here clearly have a serene quality. We also went to services in more elaborate outdoor chapels and in one magnificent indoor sanctuary, furnished from a now-defunct synagogue.

The denominational camps are not the only ones with sacred space. The chapel of a pluralistic private camp is a beautiful, open-air structure set high on a hill. Stained glass windows, purchased from a congregation that was leaving its old building, adorn the back of the *bimah* (raised platform). Both Jewish and non-Jewish staff commented that the chapel evokes in them a feeling of spirituality. The campers, too, find it a special place. A nine-year-old girl went to her counselor one day to ask for permission to go up to the chapel. She did not know if she was ready to stay for the second session of camp, and she wanted to sit in the chapel to think over her decision.

By contrast, a movement camp with no chapel holds services on benches set up on the athletic field. We soon discovered that feelings about worship at this camp are ambivalent and that worship is, in fact, an "add on," something to be fit into a tight athletic schedule. It is not surprising that at this same camp, an inter-camp sailing regatta and an off-campus sports tournament were scheduled for *Shabbat*. The campers involved in these activities were not even present in camp for *Shabbat*. Similarly, a community camp that, until recently, has paid little attention to Jewish life, has no separate space for worship. Services take place either in an outdoor amphitheater or in the one-room conference center. Since both of these settings are used all week for other activities, the services lack a sense of being in "sacred space."

Hebrew

Since ancient times, debates have raged between those who support the use of the vernacular in Jewish prayer, study, literature, and scholarship and those who support the promotion of Hebrew or Yiddish (Mendes-Flohr and Reinharz 1995; Wisse 1990). The latter clearly see Hebrew as a tool of Jewish peoplehood. In modern times, Ben-Yehuda wrote that Jews cannot truly be a people without a return to Hebrew, "using it not just as a written language for religious and intellectual purposes . . . but . . . as a spoken language used by the common people as well as their leaders . . . for all the purposes of life, at all hours of the day and night . . ." (cited in Mandel 1981, p. 28). Language undoubtedly plays a role in Jewish socialization and Jewish identity formation, as a knowledge of Hebrew or Yiddish is a characteristic that readily distinguishes Jewish children from their Gentile peers. Although children may struggle to learn to read Hebrew in religious school, they readily pick up Hebrew expressions and some degree of Hebrew comprehension at camp.

Hebrew is found in both the physical and social environment at camp. In most of the camps we studied, we could see it on the signs on the bunks and buildings, and hear it over the loudspeaker and in passing conversations among Israeli counselors. At a Zionist camp, the campers count off for an activity in Hebrew, "*ahat, shtayim, shalosh, ahat, shtayim . . .*" (one, two, three, one, two . . .) The entire camp gathers at the flagpole early in the morning, clapping hands and chanting "*boker tov, boker tov*" ("good morning, good morning") as they begin their day. Even at a nondenominational private camp, campers and staff call out "*yasher koach*" (an expression meaning "congratulations") to acknowledge a job well done.

Like *Birkat Ha'mazon*, the use of Hebrew—particularly in place names—provided us with a useful indicator of a camp's Jewishness. At a denominational movement camp, none of the buildings is labeled in Hebrew. At a community camp striving for a stronger Jewish identity, the Israeli pottery teacher made Hebrew signs for all of the buildings. These have been hung but no one refers to the buildings by their Hebrew names. At a Zionist camp, bunks are named for cities in Israel. Each has its name spelled out in Hebrew letters on colorful ceramic tiles. The bunks for the oldest group are whimsically called *"Dortn"* (over there), the only Yiddish reference at camp. The bunks at a pluralist private camp are also named for different cities in Israel. The oldest and most prestigious bunk is called "Y'rush," short for *"Yerushalayim"* (Jerusalem).

Some of the camps we visited are in the process of strengthening their Jewish identities and their Judaic programming. Toward these ends, they have tried to increase the use of Hebrew. Such efforts are often met with resistance and change is slow to come. One camp, for example, renamed bunks from English names, like the "Superstars," to Hebrew names, like *"Bonim"* (builders) or *"Haverim"* (friends). The older campers were upset by this move and had serious difficulty accepting the new names. At another camp, the rabbi and Jewish educator want more Hebrew words to be used at camp. They therefore introduce a few words each year, hoping that some will take hold. The year of our study, they tried to use *chadar ochel* to refer to the dining hall, but it did not catch on. They also wanted to name the units in Hebrew with Jewish cultural names, but that idea was rejected by senior staff as "too Jewish." A movement camp, trying to foster the use of Hebrew, gave counselors and campers a guide to Hebrew words used at camp. The guide has had little effect.

Two other camps managed to introduce some limited renaming that did take hold. In one of these camps, color war is now called *"Maccabiah"* and has Jewish themes. Unit names have been changed to Hebrew names (although during the season, cabin groups are identified by the administrative terms of "B-5" or "G-3" for boys' or girls' cabins). Many key daily activities—*nikayon, chugim, menuchah* (clean-up, electives, rest time)—are referred to by their Hebrew names, even though others, like Israeli dancing or swimming, are not.

To be sure, this "passive" use of Hebrew leads to knowledge of what one Israeli counselor referred to as "camp Hebrew." In some camps it is supplemented with formal Hebrew *chugim* or classes where there is a more concerted effort to impart conversational Hebrew. Nonetheless, even at the religious camps, directors admitted that making Hebrew a central part of camp was a vision and not a reality.

The analysis of Jewish life at camp lends support to several observations about camp as a Jewish socializing agent. To begin, camp is not a monolithic entity. Rather, there is a good deal of variation among camps, with each establishing its own approach to worship and blessings and each setting its own standards for *kashrut* and other practices. The camp setting makes it possible to create authentic Jewish life that permeates the day and seems as natural as breathing. Within that setting one can readily find examples of unfilled potential, but also examples of sublime Jewish experiences. Opportunities abound to learn from these best practices in order to enhance Jewish life throughout the Jewish camping world. Finally, as with Jewish education, staff are key to creating vibrant Jewish life at camp. Jewish life flourishes where counselors are positive Jewish role models whom campers admire and follow. We turn now to a description of the counselors at camp—who they are, why the come to camp, and how they enact their roles.

6

The Counselor as Teacher and Friend

The sages taught: "Make for yourself a teacher, acquire for yourself a friend, and judge everyone favorably" (*Pirkei Avot* 1.6). It is as if the ancient rabbis were describing the learning atmosphere at camp, where counselors are both teachers and friends, and where encouragement and praise abound. Counselors are the essential key to Jewish life and learning at camp. They create the Jewish environment, design and implement both formal and informal Jewish educational activities, model and encourage everyday practices, and turn teachable moments into Jewish lessons. But, many are just a few years older than the campers and few are trained educators.

Unless staff—from the director, to the specialist, to the bunk counselor—are ready, willing, and able to create Jewish life at camp, it will not happen. Consider the reaction of a counselor we encountered during our site visits. He told us how embarrassed he was by his own inability to provide answers to his campers' questions. He wondered how the camp could expect him to explain prayers to his campers when he, himself, did not know Hebrew and could not even follow along in the prayer book. In this case, opportunities for direct instruction, role modeling, and teachable moments were lost because of a counselor's lack of knowledge. At several camps, we found misspellings of Hebrew words in photocopied *bentchers* and on large painted signs. It appeared that the staff did not recognize the errors, the Israeli counselors did not see it as their job to correct the mistakes, and the directors accepted the errors as unimportant details. Although misspellings may be a minor problem, they symbolize how staff members can fail to maximize the Jewish opportunities at camp.

At the same time, we also met many counselors who told us that they work at camp because they believe in what they do there, "because of the magic moments of the day—seeing kids walking around holding hands, being there for each other, reaching to touch the Torah." "Teaching Jewish kids is more meaningful for me than stacking boxes for twelve bucks an hour," said one counselor. "As someone from an Orthodox background, this is much more valuable—to really teach kids about Judaism." As such counselors teach, they, themselves, grow and learn. "The counselors spend ten weeks focusing on the needs of others," a camp director explained to us. "That's a spiritually uplifting experience. When human beings focus their energies on other people's needs, it's spiritually elevating. That's a truism. And if they do it in a place that's already spiritually uplifting, you can see what it does to them. It changes them—and they become change agents in the world." Jewish camping at its best creates a learning community that benefits both campers and staff.

SURVEYING CAMP STAFF

To understand who chooses to work at a Jewish summer camp and why, in 2001 we conducted a survey of staff at the camps we had visited the previous year.[1] The survey asked about their Jewish backgrounds, their motivations for coming to camp, and their personal goals for the summer. In order to capture counselor motivation before it could be modified by experience, the survey was administered during staff orientation, prior to the arrival of campers. One camp delayed the survey until after the start of camp. Here we suspect even brief experience may have biased the responses of some first-year counselors. Answering a question about future occupation, a new staff member at this camp wrote, "after this experience, nothing related to children."

The survey was conducted in person at five of the camps; in the other camps, a designated member of the camp staff handled survey administration. All total, 1,091 Jewish staff members at seventeen camps participated in the survey. Respondents held different positions at various types of camps in three regions of the country (table 6.1).

Table 6.1. Counselor Survey: Number of Jewish Counselors by Camp Type, Region, Position

	Number	Percentage
Type of Camp		
Reform	280	26
Conservative	198	18
Zionist	157	14
JCC-community	188	17
Foundation	187	17
Private	81	7
Region		
Northeast	500	46
South	349	32
West	242	22
Position at Camp		
Bunk counselor	655	60
Rabbi, educator, *shaliach*	55	5
Activity specialist	206	19
Senior staff (unit head, director, etc.)	110	10
Other	65	6
Total	1,091	100

Note: The Counselor Survey disproportionately represents the movement camps and under-represents private for-profit camps. Although findings from staff at the movement camps have high reliability, caution must be exercised in generalizing results from the one private camp in our sample to the sixty-four non-Orthodox, for-profit private camps that operate throughout the United States.

In addition to being interested in the young adults at camp, we were curious about those who had not chosen camp work for their summer employment. Our participant-observation study had revealed widespread difficulties in recruiting qualified Jewish counselors. We wondered why there was a national shortage of qualified counselors, given the large number of Jewish college students in North America. We hypothesized that the problem might reside in young adults' perceptions of the job of the camp counselor. To test our hypothesis, in spring 2001 we also surveyed a broad sample of Jewish college students. Questions about summer employment were inserted into our ongoing survey of college students who have had contact with birthright israel (Saxe et al. 2002). Students were asked to rate the desirability of five possible summer jobs: as a salesperson, intern, lifeguard, laborer, and counselor. In total, responses to these questions were received from 4,021 Jewish young adults.

Almost half of the college student respondents had been participants on a birthright israel trip the previous winter; the others had applied for birthright but had not, as yet, been on a trip. These emerging adults, all between the ages of eighteen and twenty-six, represent a potential pool of candidates for staff positions at Jewish summer camps. All identify themselves as Jewish. Although none had previously been on an educational trip to Israel, the great majority have had enough Jewish education to celebrate a *bar/bat mitzvah* (72%). Over half were expecting to work full-time during the coming summer (58%).

Our analysis of camp staff and their role in socializing Jewish children is thus based on several sources: our observational study of camps, the counselor survey, and the general survey of Jewish college students. In this chapter, we first describe the staff structure at camp and then explore the factors that affect a Jewish young adult's decision to work as a counselor at camp.

STAFF STRUCTURE AT CAMP

Despite their informality, camps are formal, hierarchical organizations. The director, sometimes with one or more assistant directors, heads the camp. Reporting to them are unit heads, each responsible for a group of bunks defined by the campers' gender and age/grade in school. Together, the directors and unit heads form the camp's management team. About one-fourth of the camps in our national census have relatively small management teams of fewer than ten staff members. The others have up to thirty senior staff members. Senior staff supervise the bunk counselors (college-age and beyond), CITs (counselors-in-training who are generally seniors in high school) and, at some camps, counselor assistants (juniors in high school). These counselors, who live with the campers, have direct responsibility for the happiness and well-being of the campers in their charge. In addition to this central chain of command, camps have activity specialists who are responsible for various aspects of the camp program—waterfront, arts, wilderness program, and so on. Finally, given their unique mission as Jewish socializing agents, many of the Jewish residential camps also have Jewish educators on staff— rabbis, teachers, or Israeli *shlichim*.

The Director

Some directors are accountable to owners or lay boards. Nonetheless, given the isolation and intensity of camp during the summer, the directors are in full control. They serve as the "captain of the ship." They are essentially the managers of small cities and have overall responsibility for everything that happens from health and safety, to administration, personnel, communications, education, and recreation. The directors we observed handle a staggering number of details in any one day. In addition to overseeing everyday operations, they deal with the lake being closed by the health department, the chef leaving in the middle of the summer, a camper needing serious medical attention, staff misbehaving, and a spate of rainy days that require the schedule to be completely altered in a way that keeps 250 children dry and happy. In the midst of everything, parents who are considering the camp for their child for next summer show up for a tour.

Each director handles the job differently. In one camp, we rarely see the director outside of her office. In another, the director is a pervasive presence. His enthusiasm shines through each day, and he roams the camp constantly on a golf cart, stopping frequently to talk with campers or staff, who wave hello or ask questions. In still another camp, the director alternates between passivity and an active imposition of his leadership on every detail. The directors we saw ranged from efficient to overwhelmed managers, from charismatic figures to behind-the-scenes players. Regardless of their personal style, they set the camp's course and hold ultimate responsibility for what transpires over the summer.

Specialists

Some camps employ a cadre of professionals who bring expertise to the camp's program. In other camps, bunk counselors double as activity specialists. The choice between these two models is linked to the camp's philosophy regarding the importance of personal development and individual skills training versus group dynamics and social interaction. These philosophical differences have relevance to how Jewish education is managed at the camp.

For example, one of the non-Orthodox, for-profit private camps we observed emphasizes excellence in personal instruction. The camp program is based on individual choice, with each camper signing up for the activities that best suit his or her personal interests. These activities—covering areas as diverse as tennis, archery, ropes course, climbing, mountain biking, basketball, swimming, horseback riding, soccer, and camping skills—are taught by well-trained specialists. The camp buys their professional expertise and also encourages their professional development by paying for advanced courses and accreditation. The camp understands that the professionalism of its staff redounds to its benefit. Jewish education at this camp is centralized in the hands of the Jewish educators. The value placed on expertise and specialization does not, however, extend to this area. Aside from the two lead educators, the other staff involved in Jewish education are not hired explicitly for Judaics nor are they required or expected to possess credentials in the field.

In contrast, a Zionist camp emphasizes group learning, as opposed to individual instruction. It spends relatively little money on specialists, looking instead for strength in its bunk counselors. It offers minimal personal choice in activities. Rather, everything is done in groups. What the Zionist camp lacks in the quality of instruction it can offer in sports, the arts, or other areas, it compensates for by the intensity of the group experience. Campers stay with their bunks and their counselors for most of the day, moving from activity to activity as a group. Counselors thus lead their campers in every activity, including informal Jewish educational activities. This design leads to the most decentralized Jewish education we observed over the summer.

Based on the national census of camps, we estimate that at least 1,400 professional Jewish educators (defined as teachers, rabbis, and/or *shlichim*) work at Jewish residential camps in the summer. One-fourth of the camps in the census report no Jewish educators on staff. The other camps average ten educators each. A few of the camps report several dozen educators on staff although there are probably a smaller number on the premises at any one time. Camp, it should be noted, is a special opportunity for these professionals to experiment with new ideas and techniques and to reinvigorate their own practice back home. Rabbi Daniel Freelander, now a senior executive of the Union of American Hebrew Congregations, says that being on staff at camp molded his approach to teaching Torah and leading services. "Camp allowed me to experiment without worrying about the ritual committee, approval of the board, or fear of losing my job," he explains (Fax 1994, p. 52).

Camps employ different strategies to ensure the presence of Judaic specialists at camp. One of the movement camps in our observational study has six Jewish educators (including rabbis and cantors) in residence for two-week periods. Most come with their families and are called "faculty." The overall educational program is managed by a rabbinic student. At another, the entire top echelon of the camp (director, assistant director, head counselors, and many of the next level of staff) are rabbis or professional Jewish educators. In some of the non- or trans-denominational Jewish camps, there is only one educator, but this person tends to have an extensive background in Jewish education and to have great legitimacy in the role. Other camps bring in outside experts, for a limited period of time, to help with Jewish education. A local Chabad rabbi comes to one of the southern camps four times a season to lead workshops on *shofar*-making and *matzah*-baking. The principal of a community Hebrew high school comes up on Friday afternoons to help with *Shabbat* preparations. He is the Jewish authority figure at camp and also a parent figure to staff. He leaves after *Shabbat* morning services to return to his family in the city.

Bunk Counselors
Regardless of the size and role of the specialists at camp, bunk counselors usually have the greatest impact on campers. They are a constant presence for campers. They live in the bunks with them, direct their activities, and ensure their safety, well-being, and happiness while at camp.

According to estimates from our national census, at least 10,000 Jewish young adults, most of whom are college students, work as bunk counselors at Jewish residential camps during the summer. They are not, however, the only bunk counselors at camp, as many camps also hire non-Jews to serve in this capacity. The practice of hiring non-Jewish staff is particularly evident in the non-Orthodox private camps. The census shows that, on average, fewer than half of the bunk counselors in these private camps are Jewish (table 6.2). Most camps that hire non-Jews do so out of necessity; a few claim that it is a preference.

At the camps we visited, non-Jews are generally hired as activity special-

Table 6.2. Percentage of Jewish Bunk
Counselors by Camp Type

Community	
Jewish federation/JCC (*n* = 35)	89
Agency/organization (*n* = 32)	97
Movement	
Zionist (*n* = 15)	100
Denominational (*n* = 18)	98
Private	
Non-Orthodox for-profit (*n* = 64)	44
Foundation/independent nonprofit (*n* = 15)	85
Orthodox for-profit (*n* = 12)	100

ists and less frequently serve as bunk counselors. At a community camp, for example, none of the bunk counselors are Gentiles, but about two-thirds of the specialists are. The summer of our observational study, we found that the presence of several non-Jewish counselors at one camp was causing some Jewish counselors to feel self-conscious about overdoing Jewish content. Others on staff, however, saw some benefit to the non-Jewish presence at camp. They noted that the campers were very interested in those staff members and wondered why they were working at the camp, why they were not Jewish, and how they were different from the campers. "It's not that the kids are upset that they're not Jewish," a counselor explained to us. "They're just really curious to know why [the counselors] are or why they aren't Jewish."

Of the Jewishly identified staff, we might argue whether the glass of Jewish preparedness is partially full or partially empty. On the plus side, our counselor survey found that the great majority have been active in Jewish youth groups, have attended or worked at a Jewish summer camp, and have traveled to Israel. More than three-fourths feel that they know enough to be Jewish role models for their campers. They are not simply relying on what they learned in preparation for becoming *b'nei mitzvah*: Half of the Jewish staff at the summer camps in our study had taken a Judaics course during the past two years (table 6.3).

Table 6.3. Jewish Educational Background of Camp Staff

	Percentage ($n = 1,010$)
Was active in youth group	76
Attended day school	38
Attended part-time Hebrew school	56
Attended Hebrew school one day/week	37
Had *bar/bat mitzvah* ceremony	90
Traveled/studied on an organized program in Israel	72
Participated on birthright israel	10
Took courses in Hebrew/Jewish Studies in past two years	51

Note: Based on respondents in movement camps, community camps, and foundation/independent nonprofit private camps. No Orthodox private camps took part in the Counselor Survey. The one non-Orthodox private camp in our sample requested that no questions pertaining to Jewish education and values be included in its version of the survey. Questions on Jewish education allowed respondents to check all that apply.

Moreover, camp staff are distinct from the general population of American Jewish college students in terms of their high levels of Jewish involvement and in the greater emphasis they place on every Jewish value across the board from *tikkun olam,* to spirituality and *Shabbat* observance, to support for Jewish organizations. Table 6.4 presents the comparative results of questions asked to counselors at camp and to a matched sample of Jewish college students. In order to control for demographics, the analysis includes only identified Jews from the United States or Canada, who are between the ages of eighteen and twenty-six. The college student study included two sub-groups: those who had been participants on birthright israel (an intensive, ten-day educational experience in Israel targeted specifically toward this age group; see Saxe et al. 2002) and those who had expressed an interest in birthright israel but had not, as yet, had the experience.

Across these three groups of emerging adults, the rank ordering of Jewish values is virtually identical. At the top are the triumvirate of concerns of this generation of young Jews: "being a good person," caring about Israel, and remembering the Holocaust. Notably, Israel plays a lesser role in the Jewish lives of those who have not been there. At the bottom of the list, across the three columns, are the formal religious aspects of Judaism: observing *Shabbat* and attending synagogue services. When

Table 6.4. Percentage of College-Aged Young Adults Ranking Jewish Values as "Very Important"

Jewish Value	Counselors (n = 703)	Birthright israel participants (n = 1,864)	Birthright israel non-participants (n = 2,147)
Leading an ethical and moral life	68	63	60
Caring about Israel	65	60	46
Remembering the Holocaust	65	67	63
Making the world a better place	62	51	46
Countering antisemitism	57	54	52
Having a rich spiritual life	34	31	24
Supporting Jewish organizations	34	23	20
Observing *Shabbat*	25	13	10
Attending synagogue	16	12	9

Note: For every item, overall differences among the groups are statistically significant ($p < .01$).

we examine the data across the rows, we see that those who spend their summer at a Jewish camp place a higher value on every dimension of Jewish life (except remembering the Holocaust) as compared with those who do not. We also see that a birthright israel experience appears to increase the importance of these values in the lives of participants as compared with non-participants. Intensive Jewish experiences such as an Israel experience or a summer at camp might be particularly attractive to those with strong Jewish commitments. It is equally likely that such experiences are causal agents that have a strong and positive impact on the Jewish identities of emerging adults.

Finally, the young adults who work at Jewish summer camps are suffused with Jewish pride. Almost every counselor in our study said that she or he is proud to be a Jew, and for virtually all of these respondents, this is a statement with which they "strongly" agree. Jewish counselors also, by and large, feel comfortable and at home in Jewish settings and recognize a special connection with their Jewish friends (table 6.5).

At the same time, results of our counselor survey indicate that one-fourth of the Jewish staff at camp lack these backgrounds and commitments. One-fourth describe themselves in secular terms, as cultural Jews or as "just Jewish." One-fourth admit that they do not know enough to be

Table 6.5. Jewish Counselors' Relationship to Judaism

	Percentage in Agreement ($n = 1,091$)
I am proud to be a Jew.	99
I feel comfortable and at home in Jewish settings.	92
I feel a special connection with my Jewish friends.	91
I know enough to be a real Jewish role model.	78
Jewish teachings and traditions have relevance to the things I am most interested in.	67
I have serious questions about what it means to be a Jew.	41

"real Jewish role models." With the current configuration of hires, many camps face the challenges of integrating diverse staff members into a coherent and vibrant Jewish community and of delivering a Jewish message that can be carried by only a proportion of the staff. Judaically, the camps may have eight cylinders, but only six of them have sparkplugs.

WHAT DRAWS COUNSELORS TO CAMP?

In meetings with counselors during site visits, we asked what motivates them to spend their summers working at camp. Counselors commonly described camp as their "Jewish home away from home," a statement also agreed to by three-fourths of the Jewish staff responding to the counselor survey. The counselors said that, over the years, camp has given them the opportunity to "live full Jewish lives" and to experiment with Jewish practice. A program director talked about camp as a place where she can be real, with no pretense. She observed that personal growth comes from working and playing with the same people all season long, year after year. "I can learn about myself and how I interact with others," she said.

For those who have grown up through the ranks of camp, being a counselor is a way to continue their own camping experience. "There are so many other things to do and I could make so much more money, but I come here for my friends," remarked one counselor. "I don't know a summer without these guys," added another long-time camper/counselor. Committed Jewish counselors see their work as a way of giving back: "My counselors shaped me, they helped me to grow up," observed one staff member. "I want to do that for someone else." Furthermore, they like working with children, and they feel that the work they do at camp is important. One talked about teaching a child to recite the *Birkat Ha'mazon,* and how that experience alone sustained her through the season: "I could see every day that I taught a kid something new, that I helped him learn something new Jewishly."

Results of the counselor survey show that college students with no prior camp experience are unlikely to end up in staff positions at summer camp. The vast majority of the survey respondents had prior experience at an overnight camp—whether as camper, junior counselor, or staff member. This was the first year at an overnight summer camp for only 19 percent of the Jewish staff. About 60 percent of the counselors in this study had explored no other work options prior to accepting a camp job and another 19 percent had explored only one other possibility. It appears that camp was simply what they were going to do and they put little or no effort into generating other possibilities.

Money as a Factor

When we asked groups of counselors whether the money earned at camp was an important factor in their decision to be there, the typical reaction was laughter. Several explained that camping was the least remunerative of the opportunities available to them. The survey of counselors found that salary and other compensation were at the bottom of the list of reasons for accepting a summer camp position (see table 6.6).

The relative unimportance of compensation is also seen in the list of factors that drew staff to a particular camp. High on the list are the camp's activities and its campers along with an emotional attachment to the particular camp. At the bottom of the list is salary (table 6.7).

Counselors' disregard of salary, it should be noted, is not shared by other Jewish young adults. As much as counselors on the job are not drawn to camp by money, Jewish college students look at other job options because these pay more and will, thus, cover a higher percentage of their school-year expenses than would camp employment (table 6.8). Only 6 percent of counselors at camp, including those in top staff positions, expect to earn at least $3,000 in the summer compared with 33 percent of the birthright israel respondents who hold various non-camp jobs. The higher

Table 6.6. Factors in the Decision to Work at Camp this Summer

	Percentage Ranking as "Very Important" ($n = $ 1,091)
To have fun	87
To work with youth	73
To get to know people from different places	48
To spend the summer in a Jewish environment	44
To spend time outdoors, in nature	34
To gain experience related to career goals	29
To live away from home for the summer	27
To earn money	25
To get free room and board	10

Table 6.7. Bunk Counselors' Motivation for Choosing the Particular Camp for Summer Employment

	Percentage Ranking as "Very Important" ($n = $ 655)
Emotional attachment to the camp	49
Friends who were also going to work here	43
Type of Jewish experiences at the camp	41
Type of campers who come here	38
Mission of the camp	38
Activities offered by this camp	33
Interactions with the camp director or other leader	27
Location of the camp	23
Salary offered here	11

salaries mean that these students will earn a greater percentage of their school-year expenses than will those working at camp. Camp creates a dilemma for some counselors. They want to be at camp, but they also need to earn money to support their college education.

Jewish college students know that work as a counselor does not pay much. In fact, their estimates of counselor salaries exactly parallel the amounts that the counselors, themselves, expect to earn (table 6.9). Given

Table 6.8. Summer Salaries for Counselors and Other College-Aged Young Adults

Anticipated summer salary	Counselors ($n = 997$)	Birthright israel respondents ($n = 3,676$)
$1,000 or less	34	25
$1,001–2,000	48	22
$2,001–3,000	13	20
$3,000 or more	6	33

Percentage of amount needed for school gained from expected earnings	Counselors ($n = 640$)	Birthright israel respondents ($n = 3,452$)
0–10	54	38
11–20	11	13
30 or more	35	49

Table 6.9. Actual and Estimated Counselor Earnings

	Percentage of counselors expecting earnings	Percentage of birthright israel respondents estimating counselor earnings
$1,000 or less	34	40
$1,001–2,000	48	46
$2,001–3,000	13	11
$3,000 or more	6	3

a list of summer employment options (salesperson, intern, lifeguard, laborer, and counselor), they rate camp work as the lowest paying. At the same time, they believe it would be relatively easy and highly rewarding, but these qualities are not strong enough to override financial realities.

According to some of our informants, one reason more Jewish young adults are not drawn to camp is that they are highly concerned with "resume-building." They believe that other summer options (e.g., internships in law offices or stockbrokerages) will do more to advance their career goals. Such reasoning apparently does not influence those who accept camp jobs. Some 69 percent of the respondents to the counselor survey see the camp experience as an opportunity to acquire leadership skills and to take on adult responsibilities. A full 85 percent believe that their camp experience will look good on their resume.

The Lure of Fun

The primary factors luring current counselors to camp are the opportunity to have fun and the chance to work with youth. The learning and Jewish life opportunities offered by the camp experience are but secondary contributing factors. These motivations are mirrored in the counselors' goals for the summer. Asked what they hoped to get out of their work at camp, the vast majority said that they wanted to have a good time and to socialize with the other counselors at camp (table 6.10). Counselors, it appears, come to camp for basically the same reasons that campers do.

Learning Goals

Although relatively few in number, some Jewish staff members come to camp with personal and Judaic learning goals for the summer. Ratings of the importance of these goals, however, vary significantly by type of camp. Findings are consistent with stereotypes and expectations, although one might be surprised or dismayed by the relatively low levels of interest in all aspects of Jewish learning at the denominational movement camps (table 6.11). Indeed, no matter where we focus, we see that self-exploration— "finding out more about what kind of person you are"—is a more prevalent goal than any related to Jewish life and learning. It is also a goal consistent with the argument that emerging adulthood is an important developmental stage in identity formation.

Our interviews and surveys make clear that young adults come to camp because they have prior camping experience and, often, an emotional connection to a particular camp. They come to have fun. They know that they will not make much money and, like other college students, probably know they are making less at camp than they could elsewhere. The bottom line is that they just do not care. They choose camp because camp is camp and that is motivation enough.

Table 6.10. Camp Staff Summer Goals

	Percentage ranking as "Very Important"
Fun—having a good time.	84
Friends—getting to know and hang out with the other counselors at camp.	69
Leadership skills and responsibility—growing in your ability to lead, teach, work with others, etc.	69
Self-exploration—learning about yourself; finding out more about what kind of person you are.	57
Having an intense Jewish experience—seeing or feeling Judaism in a new way.	32
Jewish learning—increasing your knowledge of Jewish texts, teaching, and tradition.	27
Hebrew—learning the language or improving proficiency.	21
Zionist education—learning more about Israel.	19

Table 6.11. Percentage of Counselors Ranking Learning Goals as "Very Important" by Camp Type

	Conservative (*n* = 198)	Reform (*n* = 278)	Zionist (*n* = 156)	JCC/ Community (*n* = 188)	Foundation (*n* = 187)
Self-exploration	53	62	61	62	40
Intense Jewish experience	41	40	41	22	12
Jewish learning	43	31	34	17	10
Zionist education	22	20	40	14	4
Learning Hebrew	35	21	34	13	5

Note: All differences significant at the p<.001 level.

WHAT HAPPENS TO COUNSELORS AT CAMP?

The intensity of residential camp life that derives from the insular setting, the total environment, and the emphasis on community affects the experience of counselors perhaps even more than it affects that of the campers in their charge. Counselors' workdays are long and their responsibilities extend through the night. Campers look to them for everything: fun, order and discipline, comfort, support, friendship, and advice. In the following letter, a first-year counselor at a nonprofit private Jewish camp relates twenty-four hours in her life at camp. The counselor, an eighteen-year-old high school graduate, was assigned to work in the camp's theater program. She describes the whirlwind of activity surrounding the mounting of the first play of the season, "The Little Mermaid." Written in the moment, this letter vividly captures the essence of the counselor experience.

July 18th

Dear Mama and Data,

Enclosed, behold a *24 Hour (Or More) of My Schedule On Play Day:*

WEDNESDAY, 7 / 17

8:30 p.m.–10:00 p.m.

Tishah B'Av service. Mourn stuff in the dark. Tell campers, over and over and over, NOT to play with their flashlights. Campers appear to be deaf. Or very, very disobedient.

10:00 p.m.–11:30 p.m.

Drive to city with Sandy (head of Drama) and Shelley (other drama staff member) to get costumes for a play that is in 20 hours.

THURSDAY, 7 / 18

12:00 a.m.–1:30 a.m.

Get costumes for a play that is in 20 hours.

1:30 a.m.–5:00 a.m.

Sleep!!!!!

5:00 a.m.–6:30 a.m.

Drive back to camp early so as to avoid traffic. Listen to obnoxious talk shows en route.

6:30 a.m.–7:00 a.m.

Shower, because it is muggy and I am sweaty and I did not shower last night because I was at a random house in the city.

7:00 a.m.–8:00 a.m.

Wake up girls' side (yay!) with rousing rendition of "Under the Sea" in each bunk. We get this privilege because we were awake before the head of girls' side. Which is a rare occurrence in anyone's life.

8:00 a.m.–9:30 a.m.

Breakfast. There is no good cereal, perhaps as a nod to its being a fast day. Also, there are egg muffins. 'Nuff said.

9:30 a.m.–12:30 p.m.

Rehearse "Little Mermaid." Nearly complete one full run. But not quite. Am I concerned that a run takes upwards of 3 hours? Do I worry that we still have no idea what to do for costumes? Does it bother me that I am calling the show (i.e., I am giving every instruction as to when people go on stage, when props go on, when lights come up and down, etc.—I tell EVERY other techie what to do via headset), that it is the *first* show I ever will call, that I will be calling it in 8 hours, and that I don't actually know when *anything* is supposed to happen?
Nah.
Here, instead, is what concerns and bothers me: small children who whine, "Do we HAVE to rehearse? I wanna go to volleyball!" over and over and over. Yes, you must rehearse. Yes, I know, I am cruel. Unfortunately, that's what it means to be one of the leads in a play that opens in a few hours. Suck it up, kids!

12:30 p.m.–2:00 p.m.

Lunch. No dessert, further nod to Tishah B'Av. Carly (drama staff member) and I meet for the entire time to go through script and write things like
THRONE ON LEFT
in the hopes that I might see that in my script and call it accu-

rately. And we list things to steal from camp as props. Like forks. And chairs. And rowboats.

2:00 p.m.–2:45 p.m.

"Rest hour." Although I called 20 9–11 year olds down to the theatre right at the end of lunch, *I* cannot meet them there because *I* must meet with my bunk and a few other bunks and [the assistant director] about "a rash of thefts" committed by some unspecified girls of our age group.

2:45 p.m.–3:45 p.m.

Finally meet cast in theatre. Cast has grown bored waiting for me to appear and has taken to playing with microphones and costumes and other expressly forbidden toys. Time for a severe lecture. The severe lecture doesn't have quite the punch that it ought to because I don't have quite the voice that I ought to. Anyway, proceed to finish run and learn curtain calls.

3:45 p.m.–4:45 p.m.

Teach gymnastics. Gymnastics girls are furious that I have not choreographed a dance for them to perform. "But you *promised!*" they point out in their kindly, soothing tones. "I've been just a little bit busy," I explain.

4:45 p.m.–5:45 p.m.

Watch "Little Mermaid," the movie, with cast. Think of this as opportunity to rest, but end up getting too involved in plot of film to close eyes. As if I don't know the script beginning to end.

5:45 p.m.–7:15 p.m.

Dinner. "Finish" going through script and writing cues. In continuation of the no-dessert policy, there is no dessert. The head of programming asks at what time tonight the play will be ready, and when I answer "never," all have a hearty laugh. At my expense? Possibly.

7:15 p.m.–8:15 p.m.

Get kids into costumes. Do makeup. Do warm-ups. Preset all props because none of the kids know where their props go. And the rowboat. Can't forget to preset the rowboat. Especially because it is nearly as large as the stage itself.

8:15 p.m. – 9:30 p.m.

Perform play. Call play from backstage. Think play went okay . . . ? I would give more details, but I didn't *see* any of it. Just hissed directions into a headset and prayed that they were the correct directions and that someone followed them. More details when we talk on the phone or in person, I guess.

9:30 p.m. – 10:15 p.m.

Ice cream party for cast. Monitor ice cream intake so that everyone gets some. Soothe hurt feelings of those who do *not* get some. Walk kids back to their own bunks.

10:15 p.m. – 11:00 p.m.

Take 12-year-old girl to infirmary because she was having an asthma attack and her counselor couldn't leave the rest of the bunk alone to accompany girl to the infirmary. I don't even know girl's name. Well, now I do. It's Abby. But at the time I didn't. This task also involves trips back to her bunk to find her hairbrush and retainer for her. I ask you, am I anything short of a saint?

11:00 p.m. – 11:30 p.m.

Clean up backstage. Kids have left scripts and shorts and shoes. Don't you notice when you leave the theatre shoeless?

11:30 p.m. – 12:00 a.m.

Write this letter!

So, as you may note, this was a letter on 3½ hours of sleep, so it may not be notably coherent . . . but I love you and miss you and wish you had been there to see the first play I ever called and directed. And it is definitely bedtime. G'night!

Love,
Leila

As noted above, few counselors come to camp to gain career-related experience and many college students choose internships and other summer jobs that they believe will add to their resumes. The author of the letter matches the profile of the camp counselors in our study. She went to camp to have fun and to work with children. In the process, she learned a great deal about herself as a leader, a teacher, an adult, and as a Jew. She also had the thrill of trying out new skills in a nonjudgmental environment. As we will discuss in the next chapter, counselors may be teachers and friends but they are also learners for whom camp is a rich educational and socializing environment.

7

Valleys and Peaks of Staff Development

"The righteous shall bear fruit even in old age. They shall be ever fresh and fragrant," the Psalmist sings (Ps. 92.15). Judaism was never intended to be a pediatric religion limited to the needs and beliefs of the young. According to the tradition, the *mitzvot* and the blessings that they bring apply to every stage of life. It is not surprising, then, that camp, as a Jewish socializing agent, has as much to offer its adult staff as it does its campers. The socialization of staff operates in the same implicit way as does the socialization of campers—through everyday activities, through the environment of camp, through the repetition of prayers and blessings, through friendships and relationships with supervisors, peers, and campers, and through the association of the sweetness of camp with the sweetness of Judaism. The Jewish socialization of staff, however, also has an explicit component. Staff are hired with intention, they are formally oriented, and they are trained to serve the mission of the camp.

Given the central role of counselors, the decisions camps make about staff hiring, orientation, training, and education reverberate throughout the season in the quality of Jewish life and learning that are created in the camp community. The challenge of staffing is not just about locating "warm bodies" and ensuring adequate numbers of counselors to look after the children. It is, most critically, about having the right staff—people who are well trained, responsible, effective role models, teachers, and guides. Surveys repeatedly show that the quality and competency of staff are primary factors in parents' selection of camps for their children (cf. Rose 1998). For our purposes, the quality of counselors, specialists, and educators is the primary determinant of a camp's ability to fulfill its Jewish mission. Data from our study reveal the peaks and valleys of staff hiring and socialization. They provide a sense of how camps succeed in supporting the Jewish development of staff, but also how they sometimes fail.

HIRING

Some camps have a stable core of staff who return year after year. At one camp, we met staff who had been working at the camp for over twenty years. Another camp calculated the aggregate number of years current staff had been at camp. The total was over three hundred years. People who had started together as campers at this camp became counselor assistants together, then CITs, then counselors. Some of them went to college together and, when they were in their twenties, shared apartments.

Other camps, for various reasons, lack such consistency in their staffing. Our national census found that the staff turnover rate at the Jewish residential camps averages 45 percent, ranging from a community-sponsored camp with no rehires to a foundation camp with 99 percent of its staff returning from the previous year (figure 7.1). Camps see turnover at all levels. Each year they face the task of recruitment, followed closely by that of socializing a new crop of counselors and molding them into a community. Camps face staffing challenges every step of the way—recruiting, hiring, training, and retaining high-quality counselors.

Camp staffing appears to be influenced by socio-demographic trends. In recent years, with the Jewish youth population bubble (growing during the 1990s and expected to reach its height in 2010) and the increase in working families that need reliable childcare for the summer, camps have been filling up. In the summers of our study, camps were bringing in more campers than they had in the past. At the same time, there was a virtually full-employment economy with many summer job opportunities for college-aged students and young adults. The result was a notable staff shortage. One director observed that the "tides can turn" and he predicted that an economic downturn would lead to a surfeit of counselors looking for work and a deficit of campers with ready tuition money. Our analysis,

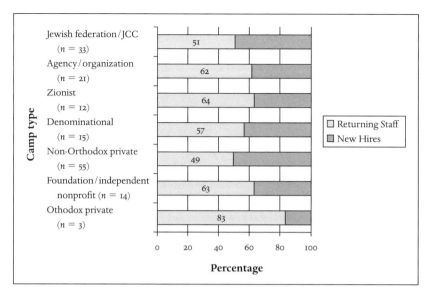

Figure 7.1. Percentage of returning staff and new hires by camp type.

however, suggests that hiring adequate numbers of qualified Jewish staff may be an enduring challenge because, for many Jewish college students and young adults, a counselor position is relatively unattractive compared to other summer opportunities.

As noted previously, the pay is low. At the camps we studied in summer 2001, staff salaries, including those of top management, averaged only $1,500 for two months of work. This amount translates into just over $1 per hour. Our national census of camps asked about the salary range for first-year bunk counselors. At some camps, that figure was less than $1,000 for the entire season—a fraction of what could have been earned working at a minimum wage job, with evenings, nights, weekends, and holidays off. Some camps permit parents to tip counselors at the end of the session; other camps prohibit this practice. Where tips are permitted, they can add several hundred dollars to the counselor's pay and in calculating their rate of pay, counselors generally take into account this additional money. Counselors are less likely, however, to consider the "in-kind" payment represented by free room and board for the summer when they think about their pay.

In any event, for college students who need to earn money for school, a camping job provides little support. On average, staff who are students during the year expect their summer income will cover just over one-fourth of the amount they need to earn for the school year. They must thus seek other sources of income to compensate for the missing three-fourths.

Not only is camp pay low but the work is hard. As the "Dear Mama and Data" letter from a counselor in the previous chapter makes clear, twenty-four hours in the life of a bunk counselor entails far more than any nine-to-five job does. What is, perhaps, most important is that a counselor gives up the autonomy that is so prized by young adults. Mealtimes, evenings, nights— times that normally would be personal downtime—are all part of the camp counselor's job description. Counselors are expected to plan and run activities as well as constantly look after their campers, day after day. They are "on" from 7:00 A.M. until 11:00 P.M. and, while the work is different from almost anything else they might do, they can never forget their responsibility to their charges.

During a site visit to a Zionist camp, we observed the counselors interacting with campers for twelve hours on a highly stressful rainy day. That evening, three counselors participated in a "paint your counselor" night activity. Standing in the middle of the arts-and-crafts center in their bathing suits, they allowed the campers to completely cover them in paint. The counselors were smiling, laughing, and apparently having a great time. Counselors need to be available to their campers at all hours. They get little privacy and little time off. Just as camp is an intensive, 24/7 environment, so too is the job of the counselor. At a typical camp in our study, counselors get two days off per session and one night off a week.

What is clear is that there is little monetary incentive for young adults to take on the job of counselor. If young people come up through a movement and have their own memories of summers at camp, the sale may be relatively easy. For such individuals, the tug of camp is great and they are eager to return each summer. These, however, are the "insiders," and their numbers are limited. The Jewish residential camps are generally unable to offer the benefits (e.g., money, recognition, college credit, access to future job opportunities) that would entice the typical college student or young adult to come to camp for the summer.

Staffing Shortages

Recruitment and hiring challenges inevitably lead to staffing shortages. One of the camps we observed in summer 2000 was short-staffed by as many as fifteen counselors. Another permitted partial summer employment, taking counselors, unit heads, and specialists for whatever time period they were available. A third asked high school students in the CIT program to move into full counselor positions to fill in shortages after the first two-week session. One camp was making recruitment calls while we were there in early August, trying to find counselors for the last session. A private camp with a full complement of bunk counselors faced difficulties hiring group leaders to oversee the counselors. The group leaders are intended to be older, experienced counselors. At the last minute, some of those hired did not show up and the camp had to find replacements quickly. As a result, three of the group leaders were new on the job and had no experience as counselors. The weakness in supervision was obvious, and several counselors complained that their group leaders did not know what they were doing.

Male counselors are particularly hard to find. The majority of staff are women, resulting in fewer male role models at camps than might be desirable. Although it represents only nineteen camps, our counselor survey suggests that female staff outnumber male staff three to two. At one camp, female counselors staff some of the boys' bunks, including bunks for young adolescent boys. In the words of a camp leader, "it may be easy to find 'bodies' to work at camp," but it is very difficult to recruit qualified American Jewish college students. The difficulty is greater still for male students.

Staffing shortages can have pernicious effects on camps. For one, the greater the shortages, the more the recruitment function absorbs the director's time. If recruitment persists into the summer, it diverts the director's time and attention away from other important work at camp. Shortages also exacerbate the problem of staff stress and exhaustion. Camps that are understaffed need to limit time off, with the result that counselors find that their free time is "barely enough just to clear your head." Shortages also make it difficult for a camp to fire counselors who perform poorly, break camp rules, or otherwise violate the terms of their contract.

With regard to a camp's Jewish mission, shortages mean fewer role models of Jewishly engaged counselors on staff—a serious threat to one of camp's best means to socialize young children.

In the long run, the shortage of qualified staff may prove to be a serious deterrent to making camp experiences more widely available. The capital costs of expanding existing camps or building new ones is substantial. Without qualified staff, new or expanded camps would be unable to fulfill their Jewish mission. This reality will make it difficult to justify such investments.

Responses to Staffing Shortages

In response to difficulties in attracting adequate numbers of appropriate staff, Jewish camps have increased their hiring of younger counselors and international staff. Some have avoided the staffing crunch by "growing" their own counselors through their movements and through counselor-in-training (CIT) programs.

Reaching down into the population. One response to staffing shortages is the hiring of younger counselors. At some of the camps we studied, the counselors were often only one step removed from campers in maturity and their understanding of how to model appropriate behaviors was limited. Some of these counselors appeared too young and inexperienced to carry out sophisticated, well-crafted educational programs that require expert facilitation skills. Because unit heads may not be much older, counselor supervision is often in the hands of people who are themselves relatively young and inexperienced. At one camp, with 120 people on staff, we saw no one over the age of thirty.

Survey data confirm our observation of camps as youth communities— young people guiding those who are just one or two steps younger. The average age of all staff is just over twenty years old. About 87 percent of the Jewish staff are twenty-two or younger. Another 10 percent are in their mid-to-late twenties. Only 3 percent are at least thirty years old. The young age of staff is reflected in their education and work experience. Half (51%) are currently in or have just completed high school and many others (36%) attend college. Two-thirds have never held a full-time job before. For these staff members, camp represents a major step on the ladder to adulthood.

Reaching overseas. A second result of staffing shortages is the increased hiring of international staff. Based on the national census of Jewish residential camps, we estimate that the camps bring in over 4,000 overseas workers each summer. One-fourth of these international workers come from Israel. On average, about one in five staff members at the Jewish camps (including directors, educators, specialists, bunk counselors, and support staff) come from outside of the United States. The total percentage of international staff is roughly the same across camp types, although the proportion of Israelis relative to those from other countries varies considerably (figure 7.2).

The camps we visited typically have ten to fifteen international counselors on staff, although one camp brought over seventy Israelis in summer 2000 to fill out its staff when it did not get enough American Jewish applicants. Some of the non-Orthodox, for-profit private camps told us that they have between 40 percent and 60 percent foreign staff, most of whom are not Jewish.

The Jewish camps commonly locate international staff through Camp America. Established in 1969 by the American Institute for Foreign Study, Camp America places more than 10,000 young people in summer positions at camps and resorts in the United States each year. Camp America screens applicants, finds them a placement, helps organize their visas, and provides support to them while they are in the United States. At the end of the season, counselors hired through Camp America receive their compensation from the camp: "pocket money" in amounts ranging from $450 for first-year counselors who are eighteen years old to $900 for older counselors or those who have previously been at camp for at least two years.

Israeli counselors generally come to the Jewish camps through the Jewish Agency for Israel (JAFI), the Honored Soldier Program of the Israel Defense Forces, and *tsofim* (scouts), and occasionally through independent connections. JAFI, the central funding agency for social welfare and community development in Israel, was instrumental in the founding of the State of Israel and in its growth. More recently, through its Department for Jewish and Zionist Education, it has assumed responsibility for a number of initiatives designed to connect Jews in the Diaspora with Israel. For example, it is a partner in the birthright israel initiative. About the same time as the founding of Camp America, the Jewish Agency established the

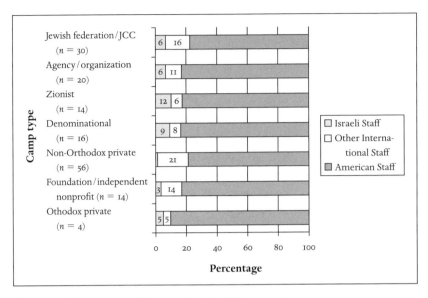

Figure 7.2. Percentage of international staff by camp type.

Summer *Shlichim* Program to place Israeli counselors at Jewish summer camps in North America and throughout the world. JAFI screens applicants, makes placements with the final approval of the camp director, and conducts a five-day orientation program. The orientation program tries to prepare these young Israelis for their camp experience, for life in America, and for their role as Israel educators. The camp directors who make the best use of the Jewish Agency connection are those who travel to Israel before the season to interview candidates in person and, sometimes, to attend the orientation sessions.

The JAFI screening process is extensive. It includes telephone interviews and a day-long evaluation workshop at which the candidates are assessed for their abilities to work in a group, build programs, think "on their feet," and present to peers. According to JAFI, those selected "are the best of Israel's young educators. They have served either in the Army or National Service, speak English well and come willing and wanting to bring a little taste of Israel with a 'suitcase' overflowing with ideas and educational materials to share with the campers and the staff at your camp. All of them are experienced counselors or have worked with children and youth either in youth movement, community centers, the Army or similar settings."[1] Such talent and skills come at a low price. The average cost to a camp is about $2,000 per staff member. This amount includes round-trip transportation, a registration/orientation fee, insurance, visa, and a $400 to $500 stipend paid directly to the *shaliach* at camp. According to a representative of the program, this relatively low salary does not create hardships for the Israeli counselors but it "definitely creates restrictions." Our own interviews with counselors indicate that the low salary makes it difficult for them to take advantage of cultural and other opportunities while in the United States and leaves them no further ahead financially when they return home.

The Israel Scouts have been sending delegations of young people to the United States since 1958. The *tsofim* chosen for this work are a highly select group: Of 50,000 scouts in Israel, only 100 are chosen each summer. These scouts, who are sixteen or seventeen years old, go through intensive training during the winter to prepare for their roles as *shlichim*. One of the Zionist camps we visited had two *tsofim* from Israel, one boy and one girl. They told us about the competitive application process and about the audition in which they had to demonstrate how they would lead a program. They said that being at camp in America was "absolutely a peak experience" and that they would miss it very much after their return to Israel.

This camp also had three counselors that were part of the Israeli Army's Honored Soldier Program. These counselors were active soldiers in elite units (two were from a fighting unit, one was from intelligence) who had received special permission to come to camp for the summer. The Honored Soldier Program was started in the mid-1980s when the Israeli Defense Forces determined that *shlichut* was a great opportunity to educate its soldiers and to give them a chance to learn firsthand how Israel is viewed in other parts of the world. The program offers participants the opportunity to serve Israel in a different capacity, not as soldiers but as representatives. It is a reward for excellent soldiers, a break from active duty. According to Ariella Feldman, North America Director for the Summer *Shlichim* Program, the soldiers come to the JAFI orientation in their army fatigues. During their briefing, they are told: "You are coming from a world that's green. We are asking you to switch to a colorful world." This switch from monochromatic green to full color, from military to civilian, from soldier to emissary, from Israeli army camp to American summer camp can be a trying adjustment.

During our site visits, we looked particularly at the role of Israeli counselors at camp and their relationships with campers and with American colleagues. Israeli staff, who bring diversity and special talents to the camp, can contribute in important ways to the camp's Jewish mission. Most notably, they model fluency in conversational Hebrew and a love of Israel. Most of them have completed their military service and thus have a maturity that may not be present in younger, less experienced American counselors. As well, Israeli young adults have been socialized in a communally oriented society in which citizens are aware of their mutual interdependencies. With such backgrounds, the Israelis are potentially ideal counselors.

The Israelis' role at camp, however, is not without its problems. In many of the camps we studied, Israeli staff have difficulty integrating into the camp community. Difficulties are especially acute at camps where the American counselors have been on staff for many years and have formed tight friendship networks among themselves. On their days off, the Americans get in their cars and go off to have fun, leaving the international staff to fend for themselves. Even if they were invited, many of the Israeli counselors do not have enough spending money to share in the Americans' leisure activities. Regularly excluded, the international staff form their own sub-community and rarely mix with their American peers.

Israeli counselors face both linguistic and cultural barriers. The Israelis have difficulty understanding—and appreciating—why American children and teens act the way they do. In many cases, they have not been trained well to work with American Jewish children, and they sometimes underestimate or disparage the children's level of knowledge. Moreover, there are problematic differences in style. The Americans often feel that the Israeli staff do not show good judgment, are too strict with the campers, and do not show the children enough tenderness. Although the Israelis argue that they have been in the army and therefore know a great deal about leading, they also admit that they do not always know how to talk about problems in "a light and easy way." Some camps try to address these issues by intentionally spreading the Israeli counselors out across the camp, as opposed to clustering them in a single unit or activity area. One camp prohibits the Israelis from speaking Hebrew among themselves in the presence of campers, unless the children ask them to do so. The directors maintain that if foreign staff want to be a part of camp, they must speak English.

In some places, Israeli staff represent a missed opportunity for Jewish education at camp. These camps fail to take advantage of the knowledge that the Israeli counselors bring to camp or to use their presence to teach the camp community the value of *k'lal Yisrael* (unity of the Jewish people). The Israelis who come to the United States are selected by the Jewish Agency from a large pool of candidates and they take part in a week-long training in Israel. They think of themselves as *shlichim* with a special mission. Once here, however, they feel isolated and under-utilized. They would like to see the camp do more Israel education, and they would like to be more involved. As they struggle for attention and for opportunities to do the work they have trained to do, they wonder why the camp brought them over here.

The one day on which these counselors take front stage is *Yom Yisrael*, a special thematic day commonly held at camps with Israeli staff. On this day, there is Israeli music over the loudspeaker, falafel and hummus for lunch, and a set of activities orchestrated by the Israeli staff and based on materials they received during their Jewish Agency training. The design of one *Yom Yisrael* we observed entailed rotating the campers through five activities, each one presenting Israel in a different way. These activities included an army simulation, a question-and-answer session with CITs who had just returned from a month in Israel, an Israel map game, a game of Israeli dodge ball, and Israeli singing. The Israeli counselors worked in pairs, trying hard to make the activities successful. All the while, the American counselors lay around on the grass, talking among themselves, barely paying attention to the activities or their campers. In their minds, *Yom Yisrael* belonged to the Israelis and this was time off for the Americans.

Directors puzzle over the question of whether the Jewish educational mission of the camp is better served by assimilating Israeli staff into the camp community or by highlighting their distinctiveness. One director wants his Israeli counselors to work side by side with Americans to provide the campers with a model of *am echad* (one people), but the Israelis want to do distinctively Israeli programming. This camp is seeking a balance between mainstreaming Israeli counselors into everyday camping activities and keeping them apart in designated roles as Israel educators. Camps that give their Israeli staff major responsibility for educating campers about Israel and Jewish culture report positive results. For example, the music director at one such camp is a young, energetic Israeli. He has done much to bring popular Israeli music to camp and to teach about Israel through song.

The generalizations above do not extend to the Zionist camps, where Israeli staff seem to have more uniformly positive experiences. The clear Israel focus of the Zionist camp helps them fit in. They serve as specialists and are very involved in the life of the camp. They feel connected to the camp and are committed to its goals. Most of them are not fully prepared for the brand of American Judaism camp embodies, with its mix of religious observance, popular culture, and Zionism. However, they find the social environment of the camp welcoming and feel a part of the camp community.

Growing their own. The difficulties of finding and training staff notwithstanding, our counselor survey indicates that most counselors are returnees who have been at the same camp previously. Those who were campers (45%) attended an average of five years. Those who have been staff (37%) average almost three years experience working in this camp. As well, about one in five were CITs at the particular camp. Over one-fourth of all staff have been at the camp in more than one role—as campers, CITS, and/or as staff—and they thus know the camp scene from more than one perspective. At one established camp, nearly 90 percent of the staff have been campers there. Other camps, new to the Jewish camping world, do not yet enjoy the benefits of homegrown staff. Some private camps, it should be noted, prefer not to track campers into staff positions. Rather, they choose to hire outsiders who bring maturity, wide experience, professionalism, and expertise into the camp.

Camps that are able to hire counselors who grew up in the movement and/or at camp cite many advantages. Homegrown staff add to the camp's strong sense of continuity and consistently high-quality counselor pool. These counselors are committed to creating the same kind of community they enjoyed as campers. The camp begins each summer with a significant percentage of staff already feeling responsible for making the camp community successful. Particularly in the movement camps, homegrown staff are important role models for the campers, as they demonstrate commitment to the program and bring high status to long-term involvement.

CIT programs, which provide an intermediary step between camper and counselor, can be an important staff development opportunity. CITs are "super campers." Typically entering senior year in high school, these teenagers play a role between camper and counselor. They take on some responsibility for the younger campers, may attend classes to learn counselor skills, and enjoy special privileges as counselors-in-training. In other respects, they are still campers. They are supervised and expected to obey the rules and regulations that apply to campers. Under the guidelines of the American Camping Association, 80 percent of the staff used to meet required ACA supervision ratios must be at least eighteen years of age. The use of CITs at ACA-accredited camps is thus limited and cannot be expanded without jeopardizing the camps' highly valued accreditation.

Acceptance to a CIT program is selective. For example, one camp accepts only half of those who apply. Criteria include demonstrated leadership skills and requisite qualities such as responsibility, enthusiasm, willingness to try new things, and the ability to carry on even when fatigued. Movement camps also require on-going participation in a Jewish educational program during the school year. Selectivity has obvious advantages but also disadvantages. Current CITs worry that rejection might cause their friends to feel disaffected and might discourage them from future involvement in Jewish life. In response, a movement camp now offers an off-site teen community service summer program that it encourages rejected CIT applicants to attend. To date, this program has attracted few participants, none from the pool of CIT candidates.

The CIT summer can be one of significant learning and growth for a teenager. At one of the denominational movement camps, for example, the CITs have twelve hours per week of intensive study of both Judaics and counseling skills, and an ongoing forum for discussing the challenges of working at camp. The director of the camp teaches this group. The classes employ a variety of pedagogical techniques: frontal lecture, role playing, group problem solving, and so on. The CITs are given the message that, along with all staff, they are part of the educational system at camp. They receive a $200 stipend for the season. More importantly, they position themselves to return as full counselors in the future.

We asked CITs at a private camp what they were taking home with them from the experience. They said that they had come to feel more responsible. They had learned to be more selfless and to put the campers in their charge ahead of themselves. They talked about comforting the younger children during a tremendous, terrifying thunderstorm, even though they, themselves, were feeling nervous on the inside. "You do things you think you will never do," remarked one CIT in the group. Much of what they learn comes from observing the counselors with whom they work. The CITs said that they had come to realize how hard counselors work and how much effort and preparation go into running activities. Above all, they reported that they had learned leadership, patience, people skills, and how to look out for one another. In sum, they had learned skills needed for adulthood.

TRAINING AND EDUCATING STAFF

Staff development is important because a camp's success depends on the capacity of its counselors to manage everyday life at camp and to design and deliver the camp's programs and activities. It is important for a Jewish camp because the camp's ability to be a Jewish socializing agent depends largely on the Judaic knowledge and Jewish behaviors, attitudes, and values of the counselors. Its importance, however, is magnified when we consider that the great majority of staff are in their early twenties, a time of life called emerging adulthood. The training and education they receive at this time can have a critical impact on the course of their lives.

For young Americans, the transition from adolescence to adulthood is a long and gradual process that continues well into the twenties. Research on American conceptions of adulthood finds that, for most people, becoming an adult means "learning to stand alone." A grown-up is a self-sufficient individual who accepts responsibility for himself, makes independent decisions, is financially independent, and has an adult relationship with his parents (Arnett 1998, 2001). This individualistic view, however, is balanced with social or communal concerns. A grown-up is also defined as a person who is responsible and considerate and who eschews risky or illegal behaviors that might injure others (Arnett 1998, 2001). Emerging adulthood is thus a time of increasing independence and responsibility toward others. It is a time of experimentation and exploration in love and in work. It is also the period in life when a person develops his or her ideology or worldview (Arnett 2001; Arnett, Ramos, and Jensen 2001). Beliefs are not set during the high school years, but rather continue to form in important ways through college and the post-college years. All of these tasks of emerging adulthood are readily confronted in counselor work.

The extent to which a person's life trajectory is set during emerging adulthood suggests that counselors should be viewed as a target audience in their own right—a group for whom camp can offer a potent Jewish experience. It appears that camp affects staff in the same way that it affects campers, through immersion in Jewish life. A majority of staff members say that camp is their Jewish home away from home. About two-thirds maintain a higher level of observance at camp than they do during the year (figure 7.3). One question is whether more can be done intentionally to direct the Jewish experiences and Jewish learning that counselors get at camp.

The difficulty is that the staff training schedule is already full. Counselors at a Jewish camp need to acquire information and skills related to the general field of camping, the specific camp at which they are working (everything from traditions, myths, and songs to correct administrative and operating procedures), group work and counseling skills, youth work (including how to discipline and set boundaries, and how to deal with issues of intimacy, emotional distress, homesickness), programming, and Judaics. Judaics, as it appears here, is literally at the end of the list. Camps generally work on all the other aspects of a counselor's job before they get to those related to Jewish life and learning at camp. Staff training programs are generally limited to the staff orientation that takes place the week before camp begins. ACA requires residential camps to provide staff orientation with at least six days of actual instruction time. None of the camps we visited exceed this minimum standard and many have a "loose" attitude that leads them to adjust the amount of orientation depending on the counselors' other obligations.

A private camp in our study offers an example of a camp that has made a conscious effort to move its staff orientation from a singular concern

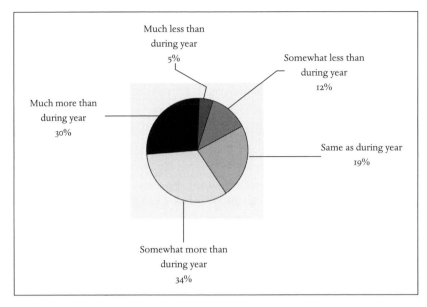

Figure 7.3. Level of observance at camp compared with home practices.

with programming and administration to a week-long program grounded in values. The camp has a canon of professional ethics that are articulated to counselors at the time of their job interviews and are reinforced throughout staff training sessions and staff meetings during the summer. By the end of orientation, everyone can readily recite the ethics mantra: "I am a professional. The children always come first. I respect my colleagues. I am always aware. My private life stays private. Shared space means shared responsibility." Not only can they recite these principles, but they understand and abide by them. During training, each of these statements is probed, practiced, reinforced. If a staff member is later reprimanded, criticism is put in the context of the violated principle. Orientation is layered: Supervisors come first and are "brought into the fold." Then counselors come and are trained by the supervisors, using various experiential learning techniques. The week attempts to anticipate all of the activities in which the counselors will be engaged during the summer. It is a time of deliberate teaching and enculturation about both the programs and the values that characterize the camp.

Training Challenges

Even in the best of cases, staff orientation programs face several obstacles and limitations. First, counselors' informational needs are a tall order, one that cannot readily be filled by a six-day orientation at the beginning of the season. During staff orientation, there is a great deal of material to cover—most of it dealing with health, safety, rules and regulations, and daily programming and operations. Camps must meet basic accreditation requirements before they can work on being centers of Jewish life, so it is not surprising that much of staff training is devoted to these topics.

One camp, with most of its staff returning from previous years, had the luxury of using a portion of orientation time for specialized subjects. But even here, the director chose topics related to adolescent development and not to Judaism. At another camp, the song leader asked to do a worship service during orientation to help prepare counselors for services at camp. Denied the request, he was told that the time was needed to give staff a much-desired break in the crowded training schedule.

Second, not all counselors are able to attend staff orientation. Either their academic schedules prevent them from arriving on time, they are hired late in the season after training has already taken place, or they are hired only for second session and are not present at the beginning of the season. One camp shortened its summer 2000 season by a week in order to accommodate the college students' schedules and ensure that as many as possible would be present for orientation. The Jewish camps' attitude toward staff training stands in contrast to that of an evangelical Christian camp with which we consulted in the course of our study. This camp requires every staff member to be present for the full orientation. Anyone who cannot (or does not) meet the requirement is not hired. The camp has a large pool of qualified candidates for counselor positions and thus has no compunction about holding a strict line on attendance at orientation.

Third, a few camps find the Jewish educational needs of their staff daunting. At these camps, so many counselors lack basic Jewish literacy that orientation can do little to give them the Jewish skills they need to support their campers' Jewish explorations. Faced with this problem, the private camp described above was experimenting with a new training design. Staff week previously included set electives, ninety-minute modules focused on different Jewish topics. At the time of our study, the director was taking a broader approach, asking staff to consider "what do you need to know Jewishly to be a valuable Jewish educator in a camp setting?" The plan was to develop and refine a new Judaics training curriculum over the next few years.

Fourth, in some settings it is difficult to conduct Jewish education for staff once the campers arrive. Counselors at one of the southern camps told us quite plainly that they come to camp to find Jewish friends and mates. When we asked if they might enjoy Jewish learning during a free period or at night, they informed us that those precious hours are for socializing and program planning. At another camp we noted a lack of enthusiasm at mandatory staff Hebrew sessions, which are held late at night after a full day of work. One educator told us that staff are too tired and time is too limited to engage in the kind of text study that he would like to do with them. The sessions he leads are limited to discussion.

Nonetheless, at several of the camps we visited, we were able to meet with groups of counselors late at night, after their campers had gone to bed and all was quiet in the bunks. Despite the late hour and the intrusion on the counselors' free time, participants in these discussions had abundant energy for talking about their experiences on the job. They talked animatedly about their trials and successes, about their campers and friends, about the camp and its program, and about their responsibilities as Jewish guides. Feedback from these group interviews was overwhelmingly positive. Staff seemed to appreciate the opportunity to reflect on their roles at camp and to share their thoughts and feelings about their work. One director decided to use our model for future staff meetings. The lesson we draw from our experience is that the negating factor may not be time but rather the choice of topic and the format of training sessions.

Responses to Training Challenges

Our site visits offered glimpses of how staff training can leave the valley of limitations and obstacles and rise to peak experiences that can influence the Jewish socialization of the emerging and young adults in the camp community. At several non-movement, non-Orthodox camps, the educators told us that the counselors, who generally have limited Jewish educational backgrounds, have many questions about Judaism and are receptive to learning. The counselors themselves told us that they would be interested in more Jewish learning at camp. Some even suggested that it be done at a staff reunion during the year.

One solution is to incorporate staff education into the routine of camp. Where the camp philosophy supports Jewish learning, we found learning at all levels: senior staff, counselors, and campers. For example, one movement camp introduced Jewish learning sessions for counselors and other staff during the camp day. These sessions, led by faculty members, are held by the pool so that campers can see the counselors learning. The themes (such as women in Judaism or Jewish values) are chosen to interest staff and not necessarily to relate to the campers' curriculum. A second movement camp found time for counselor text study by holding sessions with the rabbi during mealtime. Each day, a small group of counselors is excused from sitting with their bunks in order to eat and study in a separate, quiet space. The counselors not only have a chance to learn but they also enjoy the perquisite of a quiet meal.

While campers at a third movement camp are in Jewish study sessions, their counselors engage in parallel learning, studying the same material, albeit at a higher level. By developing their own knowledge, counselors become stronger role models and resources for their campers. Several nights a week, the staff have compulsory Hebrew sessions; on other nights they have an optional *kollel* (traditional study) with visiting scholars. Each Friday night and *Shabbat* afternoon, senior staff congregate at the rabbi's home for *shiurim* in Hebrew.

A *bar/bat mitzvah* program is offered to staff at a community camp. The Jewish programming specialists teach participating staff to read Hebrew through transliteration and to understand their Torah portion by writing a *d'var Torah* to share with the entire camp. Counselors at a Zionist camp are required to take part in study sessions on *Shabbat* afternoons. Led by one of the camp's Israeli education supervisors, the counselors come together to discuss current events and contemporary issues in Israel. Each of these models offers staff the opportunity to engage in formal Jewish education during the course of the camp day.

Another solution is to set up structures that support counselors in their roles as Jewish educators and role models throughout the summer. One example of this solution comes from a Ramah camp that has added a layer to its hierarchy: camp advisors. These advisors serve as liaisons between the camp and parents, and between staff and administration. They are an "extra" resource for campers and provide support to bunk counselors, specialists, and unit heads. The advisors are assigned to units to keep a "mother's eye" on both the campers and the counselors. They help counselors and campers cope with emotional and psychological problems. They advise on staff issues (such as how to orient and integrate second-session-only staff). They augment the education staff and advise on ways to inject Judaica into programming. Most importantly, they serve as staff mentors and role models, demonstrating by their very presence what it means to be a Jewish learner and to live a Jewish life.

If Jewish camps are to maximize their potential as Jewish socializing agents, they must resolve their staffing issues. As seen in enrollment figures and waiting lists, the demand for Jewish camps is high. But the camps' ability to expand their capacity is limited by the shortage of qualified staff. So, too, is their ability to deepen their Jewish commitment. Synagogues, day schools, and community centers face similar staffing difficulties, but the consequences for camps may be more dramatic because of the central role staff play in making camp a special Jewish experience. The camping field needs to support counselors in their own Jewish exploration and growth and to bring honor to these young adults on whom so many Jewish children depend.

8

Building a Better Tent

As the Israelites wandered in the wilderness toward the Promised Land, Balak, the Moabite king, sought to deter them by sending the prophet Bilaam to curse them. Bilaam harbored great hatred for the Jews and intended for his curse to cause their defeat on the battlefield. However, when he saw the Jewish encampment, he was struck by its layout and, according to Rashi, by the social order and the morality that it conveyed. From his mouth came a praise, not a curse: "How goodly are thy tents, O Jacob, thy dwelling places, O Israel" (Num. 24.5).

The tent is an apt image for our study of summer camps. It is an ancient structure, perhaps the oldest human architecture. The first man-made dwelling described in the Torah is the tent of Abraham and Sarah, which is open on all four sides as a sign of welcoming to people approaching from any direction. The tent is a simple, primitive structure. Comprised of poles and a covering, its construction requires none of the complex skills, technologies, tools, or equipment of an advanced society. It is a portable structure that fits into any landscape. It can be sited on a mountain top, in a field, at the seashore, or in the desert. It is a temporary structure, easily assembled and just as easily dismantled. It speaks, in this sense, of a temporary dwelling place from which one might readily move on.

Beyond the denotation of its physical characteristics, the word "tent" has several connotations. For one, it is commonly used to refer to ingathering. We talk about drawing people together "under the tent" and creating a "big enough tent" to include those who come to Judaism from different origins. In addition, "tent" connotes a sheltering, safe place. Erected in the wilderness, it allows us to draw close to nature at the same time that it shelters us from the dangerous forces of nature. Inside the tent, we feel safe, warm, protected. For Jews, in particular, the idea of tent resonates with key themes in the Jewish story: wandering, exile, dispersion, and finally, the building of a country.

These images aptly suggest what we found when we took our research journey through residential summer camps in North America. The camp communities we visited were housed in tents or bunks. Tents define the geography of the camp and its social order. The tent group forms the foundation of the social experience at camp. Dwelling together in a tent for several weeks, the group of campers and their counselors are drawn together and form the relationships—friends, big brothers and sisters, role models—that are the locus of social learning at camp. The transience of camps is an important element in their design. Children know that they have come to a special place and its time delimitation only adds to its preciousness. They yearn for camp during the school year, anticipate it eagerly as its time approaches, and mourn its passing at the end of the season. The temporary nature of camp also compresses time and amplifies emotions, adding further to camp's power to affect the members of the camp community. Just as a tent provides protection in nature, camps create a safe space in which children can expand their range and try out new ideas and behaviors with little risk.

What is clear from our observations is that much learning is possible in the compressed but safe environment of camp. Campers and counselors develop personally and socially. They gain knowledge and they learn new recreational and group skills. In the process, they acquire new feelings about themselves, the community, and, at the Jewish camps, about Judaism. Camp carries the promise of a summer of intensive Jewish life and the creation of Jewish friendships and memories. It has the means to create positive Jewish identities and to teach Jewish skills. "How goodly are thy tents . . ." captures the essence of camp and the positive outcomes that it can produce. It reminds us that the power of camp to socialize is enhanced by the beauty of its setting.

Camp's potential as a Jewish socializing agent has particular relevance for contemporary youth, even more so than for previous generations. As today's American-Jewish youth negotiate their hyphenated identities, they are likely to resolve any tensions by becoming more American than Jewish or by "coalescing" the two value systems into a hybrid that is disconnected from traditional Judaism (Elazar 1995; Fishman 2000). Whatever the process of identity building, the facts are clear. There is a rise in secularism and the number of American Jews engaging in Jewish life are, at best, remaining steady (cf. Mayer, Kosmin, and Keysar 2002). Affiliation rates are low and intermarriage rates are high. Day school enrollments continue to grow, but they still represent a small percentage of the total eligible population (Schick 2000). Most Jewish children receive their Jewish education in part-time synagogue religious schools, and their education is truncated. The majority drop out of high school religious programs, ending their formal Jewish education soon after their *bar/bat mitzvah* celebrations (Kadushin et al. 2000). These trends challenge the community to create Jewish settings that will captivate the attention of children, teach them well, and touch their hearts. Our research suggests that camp can offer just such a setting. It also suggests that, in order to fulfill this important role for American Jewry, the field of Jewish camping needs further development.

CONTRADICTIONS OF CAMP

Camp is a mass of contradictions. It is a simple enterprise that does extraordinarily complex work. Camps have strong cultures that they are loath to change, yet they have also shown themselves to have great flexibility. They are rooted in tradition but also excel at creativity and experimentation. Camp is a quintessentially American invention that, in the particular case of the Jewish camps, produces some of the most powerful Jewish experiences in a child's life. An institution dedicated to fun, it is responsible for the most serious work of the community: building commitment to the Jewish people and transmitting Jewish knowledge and values to the young generation. Out of these contradictions arise camp's potential as a socializing agent as well as its challenges for the future.

Simple Yet Complex

As symbolized by the tent, camp is the essence of simplicity. Isolated from the outside world, camps provide a setting stripped of technology, commercialism, the bricks and mortar constructions of a city or town, and the other complexities that characterize society. They minimize the normative achievement orientation of American culture and hide from sight the constraints of the adult world. The Jewish camps are further simplified by the exclusion of the Gentile world and the setting of a singular Jewish environment and Jewish course of daily life. In their simplicity and isolation, camps function as "cultural islands" and have the intense impact described decades ago by social psychologist Kurt Lewin (1947).

Yet, these simple institutions are doing highly complex work. Done well, the work requires a psychologist's understanding of the developmental tasks and realities of young children, pre-adolescents, adolescents, emerging and young adults. It involves a social worker's skill in community building and group process. At the Jewish camps, the work further requires an educator's knowledge of Jewish history, tradition, practice, ritual, and often Hebrew language. And it requires pedagogical skill in transmitting knowledge, teaching skills, and instilling positive feelings. Socializing a Jewish child is a complex task with many nuances and no straight lines. Yet, it can be accomplished well in the simple setting of camp.

Totally American Yet Uniquely Jewish

The early camps in America, founded by the Brahmins in the nineteenth century, were designed for the privileged children of the upper classes. With a Teddy Roosevelt–type spirit, the mission of the camps was to build character, impart morals, and develop physical strength and athletic prowess. Often with Indian names, these camps extolled Native American culture through the simple outdoor life, respect for nature, story-telling around the campfire, canoeing, building totem poles, and learning native crafts and skills. Participants camped out in the forest overnight and they learned how to do woodworking, start a fire from scratch, and construct a lean-to. The Jewish camps fit neatly into this mold, even giving themselves Indian-sounding names. During the first decades of the twentieth century, these camps not only offered a healthy environment, but they taught American games and sports, and served as a vehicle for Americanizing the children of immigrants (Cohen 1993; Hurwitz 1999; Joselit 1993).

Yet, the Jewish camps have also long included in their missions the development of Jewish pride, respect for Judaism, a love of Israel, a sense of

Jewish peoplehood. Their goals have always been to foster Jewish friend-ships and create Jewish memories. Camp, as we have noted, offers an ideal setting in which to create Jewish life. Precisely the same ingredients that make camp a special place—its isolation, separation from home, dedica-tion to fun, and communal structure—also make it an effective socializing institution that motivates and educates Jewishly. Jewish study is possible at camp because it is done informally, in a spirit of fun. A complete *Shab-bat* is possible at camp because there is no intrusion of the outside world. Experimenting with laying *t'fillin* or other ritual acts is possible at camp because no one will judge or criticize the learner for doing it "wrong." Prayer is possible at camp because it occurs as a integral part of daily life. Spirituality is possible at camp because camp is a spiritual place.

Traditional Yet Creative

Camps necessarily create strong, enduring cultures with all the trappings of societal cultures catalogued by anthropologists: traditions, norms, val-ues, customs, jargon, songs, myths, and rituals. As we learned from the Sherif and Sherif Robbers' Cave study, this culture emerges within a few days of the campers' arrival at camp. Its rapid emergence may disguise the fact that it is carefully designed and manipulated. Yet, it is a temporary so-ciety, intentionally recreated each year and transmitted from one genera-tion of campers to the next. At Jewish camps, this effort applies not only to ordinary camp culture but also to Jewish life: everyday Jewish practices (e.g., prayer, song, kosher meals, blessings at mealtimes), the weekly ob-servance of *Shabbat,* and the expression of Judaism in the physical envi-ronment (e.g., presence of symbols, use of Hebrew language, designation of sacred space for prayer and Torah study). It is difficult to change a strong culture for which participants hold deep affection. Embedded in tradition, the institution sends a clear message that "this is how things are done here." Campers can count on grilled cheese sandwiches on Mon-days, on color war breaking out at midnight, and on "spontaneous" music sessions on *Shabbat* after Friday night dinner.

Despite the predictability of the summer experience, camp is full of surprises. It runs on unbridled creative energy and offers living proof of the principles of creativity. We know from a range of settings—with chil-dren as well as with adults—that creativity is inhibited by psychological, intellectual, and emotional blocks. Many of us fear taking risks or have such high needs for order that creativity is stalled. Our organizations can stymie creativity, for example, by setting organizational norms that value reason over intuition, tradition over change, and seriousness over humor. And creativity can be obstructed by environmental blocks: an unsupportive milieu, autocratic leaders, and a physical setting that dampens creativity. Conversely, creativity is enhanced when revolutionary rules (e.g., "color *outside* the lines") are in force, practicality and logic hold little sway, failure is supported, ambiguity is well tolerated, and the message is clear that there is no single "right answer" to be found. Finally, and perhaps most importantly, fun environments are more creative than serious environments and humor is a proven technique for getting people into a creative frame of mind (Adams 1986; von Oech 1986, 1990).

The connection between the creativity literature and the findings of our camp study are obvious. As we noted earlier, the first principle of camp is fun and it is from fun that every benefit of camp flows. In addition, we have documented the supportive environment of camp and the ways in which it encourages risk taking and experimentation with new practices, activities, and attitudes. The emphasis on informal Jewish education at camp necessarily eliminates some of the blocks to creativity commonly operative in the formal educational settings back home. To be sure, camps have rules and procedures, but these do not feel like the rigid constraints at school. The result is high creativity in all aspects of camp life, both secular and Jewish. During our site visits, we heard new music with lyrics being made up on the spot. We saw *parashah* plays being created to express the meaning of the weekly Torah portion—plays that would be performed that one week and never repeated in quite the same way again. At a Zionist camp, we saw a flag pole that the Israeli staff had constructed out of sticks and rope, with the Israeli flag rolled up on one side of a triangular frame and the American flag on the other. When the flags were unrolled in the morning, a pulley system brought down a second large triangle that came to rest just over the stationary one. The result formed a Star of David flanked by the two flags. It was a brilliant design, an exemplar of creativity. No one seemed to mind that it was destined to be dismantled at the end of the season—just so that next year's Israeli staff could, in the tradition of the camp, build a new flag pole with a completely different design.

A unit head at one camp described an informal educational activity that he had devised to explore a key geopolitical concern in Israel. The campers made a map of Israel in a bin of sand and then, working with paper plates, straws, and other materials, had to figure out how to bring water from the Kinneret to the desert. The activity was a great success and the unit head considered repeating it on *Yom Yisrael*. But he realized that "you can't just trot out a program you have done and expect staff to get excited about it. You have to catch the excitement of planning." Such leadership, common at the Jewish summer camps, breeds constant programming innovations that seem to fuel even more creativity.

Unchanging Yet Flexible

In the curious juxtaposition of camp's simplicity and complexity, American-ism and Judaism, tradition and creativity arises camp's potential to serve as a socializing agent for Jewish youth. Our field data consistently point to the power of the camp environment and the relationships that it nurtures to build children's understanding of and feelings about Jewish life. Because it is based on fun and other pedagogical principles of informal Jewish edu-cation, camp is able to attract young people, captivate their imaginations, touch all of their senses, and guide them—seemingly effortlessly—toward Jewish practices and values.

However, our data also point to numerous shortcomings and failures at camp, made all the more noticeable, perhaps, by the obvious great poten-tial of the camp setting. Our notes are replete with examples of educa-tional opportunities that were missed because of a flawed program de-sign, inadequate resources, the inability of staff to recognize or capitalize on a possible learning opportunity, and/or the failure to make good use of the talents of Israeli staff. We saw children who seemed ready to learn fol-lowing staff who were not ready to teach. We saw negative role models and physical environments that sent ambiguous messages about the camp's Jewish commitment. And we became aware of the thousands of emerg-ing adults who, at a time of life marked by personal exploration, had come to camp but were receiving little attention as seekers or learners in their own right. These shortcomings were not confined to any one type of camp. To be sure, some of the non-Orthodox private camps are less systematic than others in dealing with issues of Jewish life, but we found many opportunities missed across the spectrum of camps—movement, community, and private camps. Is it possible for camps to maximize their potential as Jewish socializing institutions? The answer to this question resides in our final contradiction: On the one hand, the forces arrayed against change are great. On the other hand, camps have proven themselves to be institutions of great flexibility and openness to experimentation.

Forces against change. Camps cannot and will not change if they lack the motivation and leadership needed to drive change. The years of our study were boom times for camps. Many of the Jewish camps were at capacity and disinclined to expand. In strictly business terms, they had little motivation to change present practices.

Some directors believe that their formula is the correct one, that they have the optimal blend of Jewish life and secular activities to suit the campers and their families. They have some trepidation about altering any aspect of the experience, including the Jewish experience. The assistant director of one camp believes that many families are attracted to his camp because it is "not too Jewish." These parents do not want their children coming home "knowing more than they do or asking questions they can't answer." The camp, careful not to impose too much Judaism on the campers, would view with caution any proposal to enhance its Jewish mission. Other directors of unobservant camps have received few complaints about the level of Jewish practice at their camps and feel that they should not be afraid to add to their Jewish programming. In either case, camps are unlikely to make changes to their Jewish educational program and their Jewish practices unless they find good reason to do so.

Change at camp must begin with the director, who, as the "captain of the ship," sets the camp's course both in terms of its camp mission and its Jewish purpose. We commonly observed a link between the personal Jewish journeys of a camp's leaders and Jewish life and education at camp. At one of the camps in our study, the program director was an unaffiliated, liberal Jew whose own religious school experience had turned him off to Judaism. He wanted to make Judaism at camp "sweet" and believed that requiring campers to attend study sessions would only make them resistant to Jewish learning. The result at this camp was considerable tension between the Jewish educators and other staff.

In contrast, a non-movement camp widely acknowledged that the Jewish agenda of the camp intensified after the director began to take courses in Judaics and Jewish education. The result was seen in the creation of more Jewish ritual at camp and the introduction of a considerable amount of Jewish music into services and song sessions. Another non-movement camp also saw Jewish content increase with the arrival of new administrative staff, most of whom were much more Judaically knowledgeable than their predecessors, including several with master's degrees in Jewish studies.

In yet another instance, a private camp followed the path of the owners, assuming the practices of centrist Orthodoxy as the owners became *ba'alei t'shuvah* (returnees to Orthodoxy). We also met a director who had enrolled in an adult Jewish education program for the coming fall, simultaneously pushing and being pushed by the camp's commitment to more Judaic content. These multiple examples demonstrate how—for better or worse—the director's Jewish journey is intertwined with that of the camp. They also suggest that unless directors understand and value Jewish growth, they will not fully incorporate it into their camps' mission or program in a meaningful way.

Once the motivation exists, directors who try to make change will encounter the most powerful force against change: the camp's strong culture and traditions. Attempts to tamper with these may be met by the resistance of staff and of the long-time campers. This resistance was clearly in evidence at a camp making changes against the tide: When the names of bunks were changed to Hebrew names, the campers refused to use the new names. When *Birkat Ha'mazon* was introduced as a mealtime ritual, the campers limited their participation to banging on the tables, screaming certain phrases, and contriving hand motions that had no connection to the Hebrew words of the prayer. When *bentchers* were produced and handed out at meals, the campers threw them away. It is clear that directors must not only embrace change, but they must also be able to communicate the new purpose to staff and campers and to bring them along in making the change an integral part of the camp culture.

The director's commitment and skill notwithstanding, change comes slowly at camps that try to enrich their Jewish identities. After three years, a secular camp that had introduced some Jewish content still had not established any Jewish learning traditions. In several other camps, we could see Jewish content creeping in, limited by not having enough Jewishly able staff to implement the programs. According to one of our informants, infusing camp with a sense of Jewish life probably takes a "camp generation"—that is, the length of time it takes today's youngest campers to become counselors.

Rays of hope. Despite vigorous adherence to tradition, camps are highly flexible institutions. Shortly after the terrorist attacks of September 11, 2001, we attended a meeting of camp leaders in New York City. The air in the city was still acrid with the smoldering ruins of the World Trade Center, but the meeting itself was filled with the fresh air of camp. The course of world events had made the physically and emotionally safe space of camp more precious than ever. The camp leaders understood the dual concerns of parents. On the one hand, parents wanted to keep their children close to home and, on the other hand, they wanted to remove them, physically and psychologically, from the cities. Camp leaders were prepared to adjust policies and practices to respond to the new reality. For example, they considered that the no-telephone policy—that for years had helped maintain the isolation of camp and its separation from home—might no longer be the best practice. September 11 had made clear the value, indeed the necessity, of instant communication. They also talked about using their websites to keep parents informed, limiting trips outside of camp, instituting around-the-clock security, prohibiting packages sent to camp, and so on. One camp had already made plans for a psychologist to train counselors during staff orientation to recognize symptoms of trauma and to respond appropriately. The psychologist was also to be on call throughout the summer.

Most poignant for us was hearing about the camps' support of their campers. Staff had made *shiva* calls to the families of campers who had lost a parent in the attacks. Counselors had gone to visit their campers who lived in communities hard hit. They had taken them to ballgames and gone fishing with them. The camp community, traditionally limited to a certain time and place, had quickly expanded its boundaries and done its work where it was needed.

Throughout 2001 and 2002, the news was also filled with reports of suicide bombings in Israel and an unending cycle of attacks and reprisals between the Israelis and the Palestinians. "The situation," *ha'matsav* as it is called in Hebrew, had important implications for the Jewish residential camps. For one, camp leaders questioned what should be the tone of Israel education at camp. The daily news from Israel was jarringly discrepant from the fun atmosphere of camp. Do they share the news with campers or not? Do they discuss it with the Israeli counselors and *shlichim* separately? What do they teach children about *ha'matsav*? As one educator mused, "We don't want to foster romantic ideas of Israel, but also the language of crisis should not be the dominant association with Israel." Moreover, because many teen trips to Israel had been cancelled, increasingly fewer CITs and counselors were coming to camp with a first-hand knowledge of Israel. Travel for Israeli staff was uncertain, and staff who did come were likely to have emotional and psychological needs to which the camps needed to be sensitive. Many Israeli counselors come to their JAFI orientation directly from active duty, still in uniform. In the current climate, some of these counselors worried about how the Americans at camp would view them, knowing only the CNN version of events in Israel. Many had feelings of guilt, playing at camp while their friends were on the front lines and their country was torn by violence. And frequently, the *shlichim* felt an acute sense of disconnection, shielded at camp from current events and unable to tune into the news every hour as is the custom in Israel. These new concerns, it should be noted, in no way mitigated the issues we had observed in our field study: the Israelis' difficulties dealing with linguistic and cultural barriers, integrating socially into the camp community, and fulfilling their mission as representatives of Israel and as Israel educators.

The situation in Israel, coupled with camps' increased reliance on Israeli staff, the need for more effective Israel education, feedback from the camp research (Sales & Saxe 2002), and greater awareness of the issues faced by Israeli counselors quickly led to a number of creative responses. With support from the AVI CHAI Foundation, the Jewish Agency brought a number of camp directors to Israel in 2003 to learn firsthand about the Summer *Shlichim* Program, to meet with prospective staff, to attend a training seminar, and to have the opportunity to consider better ways to integrate Israeli staff into their community and Israel education into their programming. At the same time, also with foundation support, JAFI began to experiment with ways of providing more support to *shlichim.* For example, some camps with large contingents of Israeli counselors were assigned a "delegation head." This individual, a veteran *shaliach,* assisted with the development of the educational program during the winter, and helped new Israeli staff adjust to the American camp during the summer. They worked with the camp director, educators, and other staff members to maximize the use of Israel education at camp.

Moreover, Jewish educators began to develop new programs and curricula to augment Israel education at camp. The Institute for Informal Jewish Education at Brandeis University organized "Project *Mizrach.*" This conference convened camp directors and informal Jewish educators to analyze the challenges to Israel education at camp and to generate new approaches to be pilot tested in the coming summer.

To our minds, however, the most striking response was not these programmatic initiatives but rather the community caring. Just as camps reached out to families and children affected by the September 11 attacks in America, so too did they reach out to those affected by the situation in Israel. A number of the Jewish camps, often with support from the local Jewish federation, brought Israeli children to camp during the summer of 2002. Camp gave the Israeli children a respite from the realities of daily life back home and helped link Americans and Israelis at a time when the parents of American teens may have been too timid to send their own children to Israel. The director of one private camp decided not to resort to his waiting list that summer. Rather, every time an American family cancelled its child's reservation, the space went to an Israeli child.

The field's responses to these crises reveal camp's capacity to mold itself to the unexpected by adjusting policies and procedures, devising new programs, and applying the strength of the community to deal with new emotional and psychological needs. These responses were achieved without compromising camp's core mission—to have fun so that learning and growth will be possible. Camps need to apply this capacity not simply to crisis situations but also to ordinary times. The agenda for the field of Jewish summer camping is a full one (cf. Sales and Saxe 2002). It includes expanding the capacity of camps in order to reach a greater proportion of the American Jewish youth population and increasing scholarship funds in order to serve a broader segment of this population. It also includes the development of Jewish and Israel programming, the refinement of the practice of informal Jewish education, the cataloguing of best practices, and the dissemination of results. In addition, the field needs to increase the pool of qualified Jewish counselors by expanding recruitment efforts, raising salaries, and promoting camp work more widely. And finally, the field needs to focus on staff as a target group in their own right. This re-focusing requires camps to place new emphasis on counselor education and training, supervision and mentoring, opportunities for personal growth and for professional development. It calls for greater appreciation for the special talents and needs of Israeli counselors. And it calls for far more attention to the quality and intensity of Jewish experiences for all staff.

The Foundation for Jewish Camping, with private funding, has begun to tackle various items on this agenda and several communities have moved camping up on the list of communal priorities. There is rising interest in camp as a vehicle for Jewish socialization and increasing possibility that camp will assume a leading position in the educational structure of the Jewish community. The camping field abounds with creative ideas and it has demonstrated its capacity to experiment and to grow. The obstacles to change are no doubt substantial but the opportunity seems ripe. Camps are known to work magic and this may be the time for them to turn that skill upon themselves.

CAMPS AS LABORATORIES

This exploration of camping began with the story of Sherif and Sherif's Robbers' Cave study. At Robbers' Cave, camp was used as the setting for a social psychological laboratory where hypotheses about group formation and intergroup relations were tested. Although real camps are not laboratories in the scientific sense, they function as laboratories to the extent that they are places of experimentation and learning. We can imagine them as laboratories in group living, in Jewish education, and in Jewish community.

The laboratory metaphor is useful to suggesting how Jewish camping might evolve. Laboratories are settings for trying new things and learning from these experiments. In this regard, camp's potential has not been fully exploited. Camp is an ideal place in which to experiment with the possibilities of informal education. Informal education, we should note, is not "sloppy" education. Rather, it can be serious pedagogy with philosophical and theoretical underpinnings and a treasure house of methods and techniques. For example, a key to enhancing camp may be found in an increased emphasis on integrated programming. Such programming infuses everyday activities with Judaic content and leads to a more harmonious and fully involving experience of life in a Jewish community. Much of the integrated programming we observed during our site visits was in the arts or the outdoors program. These activities—which represent a creative melding of Jewish content with arts and crafts, theater, wilderness experience, and environmental education—can be models for the design of other programs. Our research suggests that such integration is possible without compromising the essential nature of camp and its primary purpose, fun.

Those who work in laboratories are expected to take careful measurements and to document and publish results. Innovation in and experimentation with informal Jewish education need to be accompanied by action research that gathers information and provides feedback about changes. Camping, like any dynamic field, needs such feedback in order to learn continuously from its efforts. To date, there has been little such research, infrequent systematic evaluation, and limited sharing of information among the Jewish camps. Jewish summer camping is, nevertheless, an important social experiment (cf. Saxe & Fine 1981), and the knowledge about what makes camp effective has potentially broad implications.

There are frequent calls for hard data on the effectiveness of camps, particularly from lay leaders, Jewish federations, and funders who seek information that will support investment in camp programs and facilities. Yet reliable, systematic, longitudinal data do not exist. Only a few studies have attempted to assess scientifically the impact of a Jewish summer camp experience on campers. Most of these were conducted in the late 1960s and early 1970s and all of them have serious methodological shortcomings. Many questions remain to be explored: What types of families choose particular types of Jewish summer camp? What influence does camp have on the Jewish lives of the children and their families? Under what conditions is a camp most likely to have a positive effect? Research from the perspective of campers is needed to complete the picture of Jewish camping and to identify its unique contribution to the socialization of Jewish children.

Furthermore, there is little sharing of information among camps and few opportunities for camps to achieve an objective look at themselves, particularly with regard to their Jewish mission. Given the more-than-fulltime nature of their jobs, directors have no chance to visit other camps in order to learn from them firsthand. During our site visits, we were frequently asked for feedback: What had we seen? What advice did we have for the camp? How could it improve in specific areas? Were our observations at this camp the same or different from our observations elsewhere? These questions were a manifestation of the camp directors' desire to know more about the field in which they were operating.

Camps are scrutinized carefully by the American Camping Association and by the local health department along all of the dimensions that make camp camp. There is, however, no comparable certification and feedback process with regard to camp as an educational setting and particularly as a Jewish educational institution. Yet these camps might well benefit from expert observers who could view their camps with an eye not to ACA accreditation standards but to the vibrancy of their Jewish life.

Given its potential as a Jewish socializing agent, it is curious that summer camps have not been the focus of much serious analysis. Uncovering the "magic" of camp is useful not only for understanding camps, but also for enlarging our conceptualization of Jewish education writ large. American culture is founded in individualism and young people today are under enormous pressures for individual achievement (cf. Bellah et al. 1985). From state-mandated testing programs in elementary school to the competitive college admissions process, our children learn early on that individual success is paramount. Formal Jewish educational programs have largely been designed in this mold. They have paid scant attention to the relationships that form among children, the value of teachers as role models, the school as a caring community, and the possibility of filling the air with Jewish song and spirit. Camps, with their expertise in creating intentional communities, can be an instructive model for schools to emulate. They can become such a model, however, only if they recognize themselves as educational settings and achieve consistent levels of excellence.

The purpose of a laboratory is to generate knowledge and develop prototypes of products that might find their way into society and enjoy multiple applications. When the field of Jewish summer camping becomes a learning system, it will know more about informal Jewish education, community building, and the emotional aspects of Jewish socialization than any other institution in the Jewish community. It will also be able to inform the design of other programs whose mission is to educate and socialize. Perhaps children's dislike of synagogue religious school and the high post–*bar/bat mitzvah* dropout rate can be reversed with a shift in focus from the individual to the collective, from the intellectual to the emotional, from passive learning to active engagement, from the teacher as instructor to the teacher as facilitator, role model, and friend. Perhaps the low level of active involvement in Jewish life during college can be countered if campus organizations adapt aspects of the camp model. In these ways and others, camp will surely assume a leading position among American Jewry's socializing institutions. And the lessons of camp may more broadly influence efforts in American society to build personal, group, and community strength.

How goodly are thy tents, O Jacob,
Your dwelling places, O Israel!
Like palm-groves that stretch out,
Like gardens beside a river,
Like aloes planted by the Lord,
Like cedars beside the water;
Their boughs drip with moisture,
Their roots have abundant water.
(Num. 5–7)

NOTES

INTRODUCTION (1 – 20)

1. Originally called the Coalition for Alternatives in Jewish Education, CAJE was subsequently renamed the Coalition for the Advancement of Jewish Education.
2. *birthright israel* offers a gift of a ten-day educational experience in Israel to any young adult, eighteen to twenty-six years of age, who identifies as a Jew and has not previously been to Israel on an educational program. Between 2000 and 2002, over 25,000 North American Jews participated in this program.
3. For a comprehensive review of the research on the impact of the teen Israel experience, see Chazan's 1997 monograph, *Does the Teen Israel Experience Make a Difference?*.

2. THE LANDSCAPE (21 – 42)

1. Sheldon Dorph, AVI CHAI Camping Conference speech. New York, N.Y., October 7, 2002.
2. Rabbi Allan Smith, United Jewish Communities 2002 General Assembly workshop on camping. Philadelphia, Pa., November 20, 2002.

3. CAMP IS CAMP (43 – 54)

1. There are a few exceptions, perhaps the most interesting of which is a camp that allows Internet access. The director, who implemented the policy over the objections of his staff, believes that the quick communication it provides helps parents see how responsive the camp is to any issues or problems that might arise with their children.

2. *Tishah B'Av,* the one Jewish holiday that falls during the summer months, commemorates the destruction of the first and second temples in Jerusalem.

4. CANDY, NOT CASTOR OIL (55 – 76)

1. *Mezuzot,* which hold prayers written on parchment, are affixed to the doorposts of one's home. *Eshet Chayil* refers to "A Woman of Valor," a prayer traditionally sung by Jewish husbands to their wives on *Shabbat* eve.
2. *Tikkun olam,* which literally means "repairing the world," refers to social action.
3. NFTY is the name of the Reform movement's youth program, National Federation of Temple Youth.
4. Reading and studying Torah (the Pentateuch or the five books of Moses) is the keystone of Jewish ritual observance. The Torah is read every Monday and Thursday, on the Sabbath, and on some holidays. When read publicly, the Torah is chanted with a prescribed tune. Total accuracy is essential. The Torah scroll is written in Hebrew letters with no vowels to guide pronunciation and no symbols to guide the chanting. Thus, it takes considerable skill to read Torah.

5. THE FRESH AIR OF JUDAISM (77 – 96)

1. In traditional observant communities, both electricity and musical instruments are forbidden on *Shabbat.*
2. *Bentchers* are cards or booklets with the *Birkat Ha'mazon* (grace after meals).

6. THE COUNSELOR AS TEACHER AND FRIEND (97 – 118)

1. Two camps from the original sample were not included in the Counselor Survey and two others were added. One private camp refused to participate; one community camp agreed to take part in the study but then failed to distribute the survey. Both of these camps are in the Northeast. At the same time, two foundation camps, also located in the Northeast, were added to the study at the directors' request.

7. VALLEYS AND PEAKS OF STAFF DEVELOPMENT (119 – 138)

1. From the Jewish Agency for Israel, Summer *Shlichim* Program packet sent to prospective camp directors.

GLOSSARY

One of the ways in which Jewish camps socialize children is through the use of Hebrew expressions. Hebrew, transliterated with English letters, is thus used throughout the book to describe camp activities. In transliterating Hebrew words, we have attempted to be consistent. There are several extant transliteration guides and our approach is to follow current common usage. The first occurrence of each word is accompanied by a translation, a summary of which appears in this Glossary. Words requiring fuller explanation appear in footnotes.

abba: dad; daddy

ahat, shtayim, shalosh: one, two, three

am echad: one people

ba'alei t'shuvah (pl.): returnees to Orthodoxy

bar/bat mitzvah; b'nei mitzvah (pl.): coming of age as a Jewish adult (literally "son/daughter of commandment")

bimah: raised platform

Birkat Ha'mazon: grace after meals

boker tov: good morning

bonim (pl.): builders

chadar ochel: dining hall

challah: braided bread

chug/chugim (pl.): elective activity(ies)

chupah: wedding canopy

d'var Torah: Torah commentary

daven: pray

dortn: Yiddish for "over there"

d'rash: homily

edah: unit

ha'matsav: reference to the current conflict between Israelis and Palestinians (literally "the situation")

halachah: Jewish law

Hatikvah: Israeli national anthem (literally "The Hope")

Havdalah: service that marks the end of the Sabbath

haverim (pl.): friends

k'lal Yisrael: the Jewish people

Kabbalat Shabbat: a prayer service marking the start of the Sabbath

kashrut: Jewish dietary laws

kavanah: concentration, devotion

kibbutzim (pl.): collective settlements

kipot (pl.): skullcaps

kollel: traditional study

l'chaim: a toast or cheer (literally "to life")

lichvod ha'siddur: in respect for the prayer book

lichvod ha'Torah: in respect for the Torah

limud: Jewish learning

Mah nishmah?: What's up?

mashgiach: supervisor

matzah: unleavened bread

mensch: Yiddish for a good person

menschlichkeit: Yiddish for being a good person

menuchah: rest time

mercaz: central meeting area

midot: character traits

minyan: the ten-person quorum necessary for performing certain rituals and prayers; praying in a group

mitzvah/mitzvot (pl.): commandment(s); good deed(s)

neshamah: soul

nikayon: clean-up

oneg: reception (literally "joy")

parashah: weekly Torah portion

ruach: spirit

Shabbat: Jewish Sabbath, from sundown Friday until the appearance of three stars in the sky on Saturday night

Shabbat z'mirot: songs celebrating Shabbat

Shabbes: Yiddish for the Sabbath

Shacharit: morning prayers

shaliach/schlichim (pl.): emissary(ies)

shir/shirim (pl.): song(s); songfest

shiur/shiurim (pl.): lesson(s)

shiva: mourning

shlichut: service year

shofar/shofrot (pl.): ram's horn(s)

shomrim (pl.): protectors, guardians

shokling: swaying during prayer

siddur/siddurim (pl.): prayer book(s)

sukkat shalom: shelter of peace

t'fillot: daily prayers

taksheevu: pay attention

tallit: prayer shawl

t'fillin: phylacteries

teva: nature

tikkun olam: social action (literally "repairing the world")

treif: Yiddish for non-kosher food

tsofim (pl.): scouts

tzitzit: knotted strands on the corner of a prayer shawl

yasher koach: Yiddish expression meaning "congratulations"

Yerushalayim: Jerusalem

yeshivah/yeshivot (pl.): religious school(s)

Yiddishkeit: Yiddish for Jewishness

Yishuv: pre-state Israel

Yom Yisrael: Israel Day; a day of Israeli food, games, and learning

zachor: remember

REFERENCES

Abramowitz, Y. I. 1998. "In Search of the Magic Jewish Teen Bullet." *Jewish Spectator* 63 (Fall): 17–22.

Adams, J. 1986. *Conceptual Blockbusting: A Guide to Better Ideas.* Reading, Mass.: Addison-Wesley.

American Camping Association. 1997. *Summer Camp Trends* [brochure]. Martinsville, Ind.: American Camping Association.

Arian, Ramie. 2002. "Summer Camps: Jewish Joy, Jewish Identity." *Contact* 4, no. 4, (Summer): 3.

Arnett, J. J. 2001. "Conceptions of the Transition to Adulthood: Perspectives from Adolescence through Midlife." *Journal of Adult Development* 8, no. 2: 133–43.

———. 2000. "Emerging Adulthood: A Theory of Development from the Late Teens through the Twenties." *American Psychologist* 55, no. 5: 469–80.

———. 1998. "Learning to Stand Alone: The Contemporary American Transition to Adulthood in Cultural and Historical Context." *Human Development* 41: 295–315.

Arnett, J. J., K. D. Ramos, and L. A. Jensen. 2001. "Ideological Views in Emerging Adulthood: Balancing Autonomy and Community." *Journal of Adult Development* 8, no. 2: 69–79.

Aron, I. 2000. *Becoming a Congregation of Learners.* Woodstock, Vt.: Jewish Lights Publishing.

———. 1995. "From the Congregational School to the Learning Congregation: Are we Ready for a Paradigm Shift?" In *A Congregation of Learners: Transforming the Synagogue into a Learning Community,* ed. I. Aron, S. Lei, and S. Rossel, New York: UAHC Press.

Aronson, E., and J. M. Carlsmith. 1968. "Experimentation in Social Psychology." In *The Handbook of Social Psychology,* ed. G. Lindzey and E. Aronson. 2d ed., vol. II. Reading, Mass.: Addison-Wesley.

Bandura, A. 1977. *Social Learning Theory.* Englewood Cliffs, N.J.: Prentice Hall.

Bandura, A., and R. Walters. 1963. *Social Learning and Personality Development.* New York: Holt, Rinehart, and Winston.

Bank, A., and R. Wolfson, eds. 1998. *First Fruits: An Anthology of Jewish Family Education.* Los Angeles: Whizin Institute.

Bardin, L. 1992. "Are Jewish Camps Educational Stepchildren?" *Moment* 17, no. 1 (February): 22–25.

Bellah, R. N., R. Madsen, W. M. Sullivan, A. Swidler, and S. M. Tipton. 1985. *Habits of the Heart: Individualism and Commitment in American Life.* Berkeley: University of California Press.

Bice, W. R. 2002. *A Timeless Treasure: One Hundred Years of Fresh Air Camp.* Bloomfield Hills, Mich.: Fresh Air Society.

Brim, O. G., Jr., and S. Wheeler. 1966. *Socialization After Childhood.* New York: Wiley.

Bronfenbrenner, U. 1979. *The Ecology of Human Development: Experiments by Nature and Design.* Cambridge: Harvard University Press.

Brown, R. 1986. *Social Psychology.* 2d ed. New York: The Free Press.

Bugental, D. B., and J. J. Goodnow. 1997. "Socialization Processes." In *Handbook of Child Psychology,* ed. W. Damon, 5th ed., vol. 3, 389–462. New York: Wiley.

Chazan, B. 1997. *Does the Teen Israel Experience Make a Difference?* New York: Israel Experience, Inc.

———. 1991. "What Is Informal Jewish Education?" *Journal of Jewish Communal Service* 67, no. 4: 300–308.

Cohen, B. I. 1989. "A Brief History of the Ramah Movement." In *The Ramah Experience: Community and Commitment,* ed. S. C. Ettenberg and G. Rosenfield, 3–16. New York: The Jewish Theological Seminary of America.

Cohen, D. 1993. "Outdoor Sojourn: A Brief History of Summer Camp in the United States." In *A Worthy Use of Summer,* ed. J. W. Joselit, 10–14. Philadelphia: National Museum of American Jewish History.

Cohen, E. H. 1994. *Towards a Strategy of Excellence: A Structural Analysis.* Jerusalem: The Joint Authority for Jewish Zionist Education, Youth and Hechalutz Department.

———. 1995. *The Participants of the Israel Experience Short-term Programs, Summer 1994.* Jerusalem: The Joint Authority for Jewish Zionist Education, Youth and Hechalutz Department.

Cohen, S. M. 2000. "Assessing the Vitality of Conservative Judaism in North America: Evidence from a Survey of Synagogue Members." In *Jews in the Center: Conservative Synagogues and their Members,* ed. J. Wertheimer, 13–65. New Brunswick, N.J.: Rutgers University Press.

———. 1999. "Camp Ramah and Adult Jewish Identity." In *Ramah: Reflections at Fifty: Visions for a New Century,* ed. S. A. Dorph, 95–129. New York. National Ramah Commission.

———. 1995. "The Impact of Varieties of Jewish Education upon Jewish Identity: An Inter-generational Perspective." *Contemporary Jewry* 16: 68–96.

Cohen, S. M., and A. Eisen. 2000. *The Jew Within: Self, Family and Community in America.* Bloomington: Indiana University Press.

Cohen, S. M., L. Fein, and S. Israel. 2000. *Meaningful Jewish Community.* New York: Florence G. Heller-JCC Association Research Center.

Commission on Jewish Education in North America. 1991. *A Time to Act.* Lanham, Md.: University Press of America.

Craig, W., ed. 2000. *Childhood Social Development: The Essential Readings.* Malden, Mass.: Blackwell Publishers.

Dewey, J. 1964. *Democracy and Education.* New York: Macmillan.

Dorph, S. A., ed. 1999. *Ramah Reflections at Fifty: Visions for a New Century.* New York: National Ramah Commission.

Eisen, A. 1992. "Theology and Community." In *Imagining the Jewish Future,* ed. D. A. Teutsch, 247–76. Albany: State University of New York Press.

———. 1990. "The Rhetoric of Chosenness and the Fabrication of American Jewish Identity." In *American pluralism and the Jewish community,* ed. S. M. Lipset, 53–69. New Brunswick, N.J.: Transaction Publishers.

Elazar, D. J. 1995. "The Future of American Jewry." *Contemporary Jewry* 16: 110–21.

Erikson, E. H. 1968. *Identity, Youth and Crisis.* New York: W. W. Norton.

Fax, J. G. 1994. "Jewish Summer Camps: Making *Machers.*" *Moment* 19, no. 1: 50–52.

Fazio, R. H., and M. P. Zanna. 1981. "Direct Experience and Attitude-Behavior Consistency." In *Advances in Experimental Social Psychology,* ed. L. Berkowitz, vol. XIV, 161–202. New York: Academic Press.

Fehrenbach, P. A., D. J. Miller, and M. H. Thelen. 1979. "The Importance of Consistency in Modeling Behavior upon Imitation: A Comparison of Single and Multiple Models." *Journal of Personality and Social Psychology* 37: 1412–17.

Fishman, S. B. 2000. *Jewish Life and American Culture.* Albany: State University of New York.

Foundation for Jewish Camping. 1999. *Directory of Jewish Camps*. New York: Foundation for Jewish Camping.

Fox, S., with W. Novak. 1997. *Vision at the Heart: Lessons from Camp Ramah on the Power of Ideas in Shaping Educational Institutions*. New York: Council for Initiatives in Jewish Education.

Garbarino, J., K. Kostelny, and F. Barry. 1997. "Value Transmission in an Ecological Context: The High-risk Neighborhood." In *Parenting and Children's Internalization of Values: A Handbook of Contemporary Values*, ed. J. E. Grusec and L. Kuczynski, 307–32. New York: Wiley.

Gladwell, M. 2000. *The Tipping Point: How Little Things Can Make a Big Difference*. Boston: Little, Brown and Company.

Goldberg, H., S. Heilman, and B. Kirshenblatt-Gimblett. 2002. *The Israel Experience: Studies in Jewish Identity and Youth Culture*. New York: The Andrea and Charles Bronfman Philanthropies.

Goldstein, S. 1992. "Profile of American Jewry: Insights from the 1990 National Jewish Population Survey." In *American Jewish Year Book*, ed. D. Singer, vol. 92, 77–173. New York: The American Jewish Committee.

Goldstein, S., and A. Goldstein. 1995. *Jews on the Move: Implications for Jewish Identity*. Albany: State University of New York Press.

Goslin, D. A., ed. 1969. *Handbook of Socialization Theory and Research*. Chicago: Rand McNally College Publishing Co.

Grolnick, W. S., E. L. Deci, and R. M. Ryan. 1997. "Internalization within the Family: The Self-determination Theory Perspective." In *Parenting and Children's Internalization of Values: A Handbook of Contemporary Values*, ed. J. E. Grusec and L. Kuczynski, 135–61. New York: Wiley.

Grusec, J. E., and L. Kuczynski, eds. 1997. *Parenting and Children's Internalization of Values: A Handbook of Contemporary Values*. New York: Wiley.

Haan, N. 1985. "Processes of Moral Development: Cognitive or Social Disequilibrium?" *Developmental Psychology* 21, 6: 996–1006.

Harris, J. R. 1995. "Where Is the Child's Environment? A Group Socialization Theory of Development," *Psychological Review* 102, no. 3: 458–89.

Heilman, S. 1992. "Inside the Jewish School." In *What We Know about Jewish Education*, ed. S. L. Kelman, 311–12. Los Angeles: Torah Aura.

Hoffman, L. A. 2002. *The Journey Home: Discovering the Deep Spiritual Wisdom of the Jewish Tradition*. Boston: Beacon Press.

———. 1987. *Beyond the Text*. Bloomington: Indiana University Press.

———. 1980. "The Synagogue, the Havurah and Liable Communities, *Response* 38: 37–41.

Hoffman, L. A., and R. Wolfson. 1999. "The Vision of Synagogue 2000." *Contact* 2, no. 1: 6–7.

Holtz, B. 1993. *Best Practices Project: The Supplementary School.* Cleveland: Council for Initiatives in Jewish Education.

Horowitz, B. 2000. *Connections and Journeys: Assessing Critical Opportunities for Enhancing Jewish Identity.* New York: UJA-Federation of New York, Commission on Jewish Identity & Renewal.

Hurwitz, D. L. 1999. "How Lucky We Were." *American Jewish History* 87, no. 1: 30–59.

Israel, S., and D. Mittelberg. 1998. *The Israel Visit–Not Just for Teens: The Characteristics and Impact of College-age Travel to Israel.* Waltham, Mass.: Brandeis University, Cohen Center for Modern Jewish Studies.

Joselit, J. W. 1993. "The Jewish Way of Play." In *A Worthy Use of Summer: Jewish Summer Camping in America,* ed. J. W. Joselit, 15–28. Philadelphia: National Museum of American Jewish History.

Kadushin, C., S. Kelner, and L. Saxe. 2000. *Being a Jewish Teenager in America: Trying to Make It.* Waltham, Mass.: Brandeis University, Cohen Center for Modern Jewish Studies.

Kaplan, M. 1934. *Judaism as Civilization: Toward a Reconstruction of American Jewish Life.* New York: Macmillan.

Kelman, H. C. 1961. "Processes of Opinion Change." *Public Opinion Quarterly* 25: 57–78.

Keysar, A., B. A. Kosmin, and J. Scheckner. 2000. *The Next Generation: Jewish Children and Adolescents.* Albany: State University of New York Press.

Kosmin, B. A., S. Goldstein, J. Waksberg, N. Lerer, A. Keysar, and J. Scheckner. 1991. *Highlights of the CJF 1990 National Jewish Population Survey.* New York: Council of Jewish Federations.

Kuczynski, L., S. Marshall, and K. Schell. 1997. "Value Socialization in a Bi-directional Context." In *Parenting and Children's Internalization of Values: A Handbook of Contemporary Values,* ed. J. E. Grusec and L. Kuczynski, 23–50. New York: Wiley.

Lewin, K. 1947. "Frontiers in Group Dynamics." *Human Relations* 1: 2–38.

Lipset, S. M., and E. Raab. 1995. *Jews and the New American Scene.* Cambridge: Harvard University Press.

Mandel, G. 1981. "*Sheelah Nikhbadah* and the Revival of Hebrew." In *Eliezar Ben-Yehudah: A Symposium in Oxford,* ed. E. Silberschlag, 25–39. Oxford: The Oxford Centre for Postgraduate Hebrew Studies.

Marsh, P. E. 2000. *What Does Camp Do for Kids?* Martinsville, Ind.: American Camping Association.

Martin, P., and M. A. Smyer. 1990. "The Experience of Micro- and Macroevents: A Life Span Analysis." *Research on Aging* 12: 294–310.

Mayer, E., B. Kosmin, and A. Keysar. 2002. *American Jewish Identity Survey 2001: An Exploration in Demography and Outlook of a People.* New York: Graduate Center of the City University of New York.

Mendes-Flohr, P., and J. Reinharz, eds. 1995. *The Jew in the Modern World: A Documentary History.* New York: Oxford University Press.

Mittelberg, D. 1999. *The Israel Connection and American Jews.* Westport, Conn.: Praeger.

Mono, B. 2001. "Does Camp Matter? Examining the Impact of Summer Days on Jewish Lives." *Jewish Exponent* 209, no. 26: cover, 8.

Nelson, J., and F. E. Aboud. 1985. "The Resolution of Social Conflict between Friends." *Child Development* 56: 1009–17.

Popkin, H. M. 1997. *"Once upon a summer." Blue Star Camps: 50 Years of Memories.* Hollywood, Fla.: Blue Star Camps, Inc.

Potok, C. 1993. "A Worthy Use of Summer: Introduction." In *A Worthy Use of Summer: Jewish Summer Camping in America,* ed. J. W. Joselit, 5–8. Philadelphia: National Museum of American Jewish History.

Prell, R. 2000. "Communities of Choice and Memory: Conservative Synagogues in the Late Twentieth Century." In *Jews in the Center: Conservative Synagogues and their Members,* ed. J. Wertheimer, 269–358. New Brunswick, N.J.: Rutgers University Press.

Putnam, R. D. 2000. *Bowling Alone: The Collapse and Revival of American Community.* New York: Simon & Schuster.

Reisman, B. 1978. *The Jewish Experiential Book.* Hoboken, N.J.: Ktav Publishing.

———. 1990. *Informal Jewish Education in North America.* Report to the Commission on Jewish Education in North America. Cleveland: Mandel Associated Foundations and Jewish Education Service of North America.

———. 1993. *Adult Education Trips to Israel: A Transforming Experience.* Jerusalem: Melitz Center for Jewish-Zionist Education.

Rose, R. L. 1998. "Staff Development: The Foundation of a Quality Program." In *Camp Is Business: Pathways to a Successful Future,* ed. C. B. Rotman, 71–83. Wellesley, Mass.: Babson Press.

Sales, A. 1999. *Israel Experience: Testing the Four-Week Option.* Unpublished manuscript.

Sales, A. L., A. Koren, and S. L. Shevitz. 2000. *Sh'arim: Building Gateways to Jewish Life and Community.* Boston: Commission on Jewish Continuity.

Sales, A. L., and L. Saxe. 2002. *Limud by the Lake: Fulfilling the Educational Potential of Jewish Summer Camps.* New York: The AVI CHAI Foundation.

Sarna, J. D. 2001. *The Crucial Decade in Jewish Camping.* Unpublished manuscript.

Saxe, L., and M. Fine. 1981. *Social Experiments: Methods for Design and Evaluation.* Newbury Park, Calif.: Sage.

Saxe, L., C. Kadushin, S. Kelner, M. Rosen, and E. Yereslove. 2002. *A Mega-Experiment in Jewish Education: The Impact of birthright israel.* Waltham, Mass.: Brandeis University, Cohen Center for Modern Jewish Studies.

Schick, M. 2000. *A Census of Jewish Day Schools in the United States.* New York: The AVI CHAI Foundation.

Schiff, A. I., and M. Schneider. 1994. "Far-reaching Effects of Extensive Jewish Day School Attendance: The Impact of Jewish Education on Jewish Behavior and Attitudes." Research Report 2. New York: Yeshiva University, Azrieli Graduate Institute of Jewish Education and Administration.

Shabi, M., and W. W. El Ansari. 2001. "Leaders' Perceptions of Youth Identity in a Summer Camp in the United Kingdom: A Qualitative Enquiry." *European Judaism* 34, no. 1: 142–57.

Sherif, M., O. J. Harvey, B. J. White, W. R. Hood, and C. W. Sherif. 1961. *Intergroup Conflict and Cooperation: The Robbers' Cave Experiment.* Norman: Institute of Group Relations, The University of Oklahoma.

Sherif, M., and C. W. Sherif. 1953. *Groups in Harmony and Tension.* New York: Harper & Row.

Taskforce on Congregational and Communal Jewish Education. 2000. *A Vision for Excellence.* New York: Jewish Education Service of North America, Inc.

Tobin, G. A., and M. Weinstein. 2000. *Jewish Camping.* San Francisco: Institute for Jewish & Community Research.

U.S. Bureau of the Census. 1998. *Statistical Abstracts of the United States.* Washington, D.C.: U.S. Bureau of the Census.

von Oech, R. 1990. *A Whack on the Side of the Head: How You Can Be More Creative.* New York: Warner Books, Inc.

———. 1986. *A Kick in the Seat of the Pants: Using your Explorer, Artist, Judge and Warrior To Be More Creative.* New York: Perennial Library.

Wertheimer, J. 1999. "Jewish Education in the United States: Recent Trends and Issues." In *American Jewish Year Book 1999,* ed. D. Singer, vol. 99, 3–115. New York: The American Jewish Committee.

Wisse, R. R. 1990. "The Hebrew Imperative." *Commentary* (June): 34–39.

Wolfson, R. nd. "Synagogues: Now and Soon." In *Partnerships for a New Vision: Sacred Community, Kehillah Kedoshah.* New York: Synagogue 2000.

Yoffie, E. 2001. *Sermon by Rabbi Eric Yoffie at the Boston Biennial.* New York: Union of American Hebrew Congregations.

Zeldin, M. 1989. "Understanding Informal Jewish Education: Reflections on the Philosophical Foundations of NFTY." *Journal of Reform Judaism* 36, no. 4: 26–34.

INDEX

Tables are represented with a page number followed by a "t."

130; selection process, 131; and self-development, 131; and skills needed for adulthood, 131–32; and staff shortages, 124

creativity, 143–45

cultural arts, Jewish: at Blue Star, 27; and failure to create opportunity, 73; and integration of Jewish education, 60, 152. *See also* drama; education, Jewish; religious practices at camp; singing

cultural barriers and Israeli staff, 128

"cultural islands," 46, 142

culture of camp: definition of, 49; diversity by region, 30; influence of sponsorship on, 24; traditional versus flexible, 141, 143–45

curriculum: and decentralization of Jewish education, 62; examples of, 68; experimentation at camp, 10, 67, 103, 143, 151; hidden versus overt, 10; at movement camps, 67

customs. *See* rituals and customs at camp

D

daily prayers. See *t'fillot*

day schools. *See* Jewish day schools

days off for staff, 122

decentralization of Jewish education. *See* education, Jewish

denominational camps: 26, 32. *See also* movement camps

Department for Jewish and Zionist Education, 125

direct experience. *See* experiential learning

directors, camp, 78, 99, 101, 146–47, 149, 153

disrespect. *See* inappropriate behaviors

diversity among Jewish camps, 21–23, 40–41, 56, 87–90, 95

Dorph, Rabbi Sheldon, 32

drama: description of counselor's work in, 113–16; and engagement of campers in *Tishah B'Av*, 90–91; and failure to create opportunity, 73; and integration of Jewish education, 60, 144, 152

d'rash (homily) on the *parashah* and engagement of campers, 82

E

earnings. *See* compensation

education, formal Jewish: aspects of, 10–11, 63–65; compulsory nature, 62; and "hidden curriculum," 10; staff engagement in, 137

education, informal Jewish: aspects of, 10–11, 55, 66; and creativity, 144; definition of, 151–52; as effective socializing agent, 143, 151, 153; and "emergent outcomes," 63; and fun, 145; and professionalism, 11; voluntary nature of, 62. *See also* experiential learning

education, Jewish: and assimilation of Israeli staff, 129; at Blue Star, 27; centralization of, 61–62; compartmentalization of, 58–59; and counselors-in-training (CITs), 131; and counselors' role, 98; decentralization of, 62, 102; degree of, 36, 38, 39t, 56, 95, 151; evaluation of, 68–74, 152–53; explicit versus implicit, 23, 27; girls more engaged than boys, 73; improvements to foster, 139–54; integration of, 58–59, 152; and missed learning opportunities, 72–75, 98, 129, 145–46; and motivation to be a counselor, 111, 112t; passive, 91; as purpose of camp, 26; reform and improvement of, 9; by religious schools, 8–9; and staff training, 135–36. *See also* education, formal Jewish; education, informal Jewish; socializing agent, Jewish

educational goals. *See* goals, educational

educators, Jewish, 99t, 101–3, 150

"emergent outcomes" and goals of informal education, 63

Hashomer Hatsair, 25

Hasidic camps, 23

Hatikvah (Israel national anthem), 40, 51

Havdalah service, 37–38, 80

health and safety, 47, 103, 140, 148

Hebrew: *chug* as example of formal education, 65; and identity formation, 93; as indicator of camp's Jewishness, 93; and Israeli staff, 128–29; learning as motivator to be a counselor, 112t; mandatory training for staff, 136–37; misspellings of, 97–98; promotion of, 93–94, 143

Hebrew school and staff background, 105

hierarchical structure. *See* organizational structure

"Hinei Ma Tov," 80

Holocaust remembrance, 90, 106t

homegrown staff. *See* counselors-in-training (CITs)

Honored Soldier Program of the Israel Defense Forces, 125, 127

"How goodly are thy tents," 139, 154

I

identification and social influence, 13

identity formation: and camper-camper relations, 15; and centralization of Jewish education, 61–62; and emerging adulthood, 16, 111, 132–33; positive Jewish, 140; and rise of secularism, 141; and role of Hebrew, 93; and socialization, 4, 13. *See also* Jewish identity

ideology, 24

imitation and social learning, 14, 71–72

immersion experience. *See* total environment

inappropriate behaviors, counselors as role models for, 72, 80–81

"in-kind" payment and staff compensation, 121

inclusion criteria, in census, 22–23

individuation, definition of, 4–5

influence, social. *See* socialization

informal education. *See* education, informal Jewish

Institute for Informal Jewish Education, 11

integration of Israeli counselors. *See* Israeli staff, integration of

integration of Jewish education. *See* education, Jewish

interdisciplinary approach to study, 18

internalization and social influence, 13–14, 15

international staff. *See* Israeli staff

Internet access at camp, 47, 155n

interpersonal skills: derived from camp, 13, 45, 49; and socialization processes, 13. *See also* socialization

intimacy. *See* community, sense of

isolated setting, 1, 46–48, 113, 141–42

Israel: connection to at camp, 36, 39; education about, 129; feelings toward by staff, 106t; identification with, 11; love of, 128, 142

Israel and Zionist activities, 40

Israel experience: impact of, 11–12; importance of to camp staff, 39, 105; as informal education, 10–11; participation in, 17, 40, 68, 105, 149; research on, 155n

Israel Experience, Inc., 11

Israeli children and attendance at camp, 150

Israeli Defense Forces, 125, 127

Israeli flag and creativity, 144–45

Israeli national anthem, 40, 51

Israeli staff: and camp's Jewish mission, 128–29; compensation for, 127; differences from American staff, 128; increase in hiring of, 35, 125–30, 149; integration of, 128–29, 149, 151; screening and placement of, 126; training of, 129

middle-class institution, camping as a, 27

Middle East, security in and teen trips to Israel, 39, 68. *See also* birthright israel

midot (traits), 57, 67

minyan (praying in a group), 5, 50. See also *t'fillot* (daily prayers)

missed opportunities. *See* education, Jewish

mission of camp. *See* goals of camp

models. *See* role modeling

monetary incentive. *See* compensation

motivation to be a counselor: and career goals, 109t; and compensation, 108–11, 121–22; and emotional attachment to particular camp, 108–9; and free room and board, 109t; friendship as a, 107, 109, 112t; and fun, 98, 109t, 111, 112t; and geographic distribution of camps, 109; and goals of camp, 109, 111–12; and group development, 107; and Jewish environment, 109t, 111, 112t; and nature, 109t; and personal development, 98, 106t, 109–11, 112t; and Zionist education, 112t

movement camps: about, 25–26; and capacity and Jewish campers served, 33t; and costs of camp, 36; and Jewish education, 39t, 59–62, 67; examples of goals, 57; and homegrown staff, 130–131; and interest in Judaism, 111; and Israel/Zionist activities, 40; and number of staff, 35t; and religious practices, 37. *See also* denominational camps; Zionist camps

N

National Council of Synagogue Youth (NCSY), 26

National Federation of Temple Youth (NFTY), 67, 156n

National Ramah, 32. *See also* Ramah

nature: 47, 61, 109t. *See also* environmentalism; *teva* (nature) program

new behaviors: 16, 71–72, 91, 117, 140, 151. *See also* experimentation at camp

new camps, decisions on where to situate, 30

non-Jewish staff, 103–4

non-kosher food *(treif)*, 86

non-Orthodox for-profit camps: and costs of camp, 36; dominance of, 41; and engagement in Jewish practices, 41, 145; growing presence of, 26–27; and international staff, 125; and non-Jewish staff, 103–4; and percentage of Jewish campers, 32; and scholarships from, 36. *See also* private camps

North American Alliance, 11

number of Jewish campers. *See* population, Jewish camper

number of Jewish camps. *See* census of Jewish camps

O

observance, at camp versus home, 133, 134t

observance of *Shabbat*. See *Shabbat*

opportunities, missed. *See* education, Jewish

organizational structure, 24, 100–101, 124

orientation of staff. *See* staff training

Orthodox for-profit camps: 28, 57. *See also* private camps

Orthodox organizations and camp scholarships, 25

Orthodox youth movement. *See* National Council of Synagogue Youth

P

parents' access to camp, 3, 47

parents as socializing agents, 7–8

pay. *See* compensation

peer socialization. *See* socialization

peoplehood, 5. See also *k'lal Yisrael* (the Jewish people)

personal development as motivation to be a counselor, 98, 106t, 107, 109–11, 112t

philosophy of camp. *See* goals of camp

Popkin, Harry and Herman, 27

population bubble, Jewish youth, 120

population, Jewish camper, 30, 31t, 32–33. *See also* census of Jewish camps

post-*bar/bat mitzvah* dropout, 141, 154

Potok, Chaim, 25–26

prayers, morning, 53. See also *t'fillot* (daily prayers)

praying in a group, 5, 50. See also *t'fillot* (daily prayers)

pride, Jewish, 106, 107t

private camps: about, 24, 26–28; and capacity and Jewish campers served, 33t; and cost of camp, 36; examples of goals, 57; and incorporation of Jewish education, 39t; and number of Jewish campers, 32; and number of staff, 35t; and religious practices, 37; and return rate, 32, 130; in separate economic tier, 28. *See also* non-Orthodox for-profit camps; Orthodox for-profit camps

professionalism: and informal Jewish education, 11; of staff, 102, 142

profit motive and incorporation of Jewish education, 38–39, 41

purpose of camp. *See* goals of camp

Putnam, Robert, 6

R

rabbis. *See* educators, Jewish

Ramah, 26, 32, 57, 59

recharging at camp, 33, 102

recreational skills derived from camp, 45

Reform movement. *See* Union of American Hebrew Congregations

region, camps by. *See* geographic distribution of camps

regulations, camp. *See* standards

Reisman, Bernard, 63–64

relationships at camp. *See* socialization

religious practices: effect of Israel experience on, 12; inconsistencies in, 78

religious practices at camp, 36–40, 78–83. *See also* education, Jewish

religious school, 8–9, 23, 49, 63, 154

return rate: benefits of having high, 46; of campers, 34t; and commitment of staff, 131; and counselors-in-training (CITs), 132; improving, 151; at private camps, 32; of staff, 120, 121t, 130

review process. *See* American Camping Association (ACA)

rewards used to gain compliance, 15

rituals and customs at camp, 1, 49–50, 77, 78, 82

Robbers' Cave experiment, 1–4, 143, 151

role modeling: for camp staff, 138; counselors as source for social learning, 14–15, 71–72; effect of staff shortages on, 124; effective, 119; and hiring younger staff, 124; and knowledge of Judaism, 104, 107; and singing of *Birkat Ha'mazon*, 87; during *t'fillot*, 80–81

room and board. *See* "in-kind" payment and staff compensation

ruach (spirit), 17

S

"sacred communities," 7

sacred space, 92–93, 143

safety, sense of at camp, 47, 103, 140, 148. *See also* standards

salary. *See* compensation

scholarships, 25, 35–36, 150

schools as socializing agents, 8–10

scouts *(tsofim)*, 125, 127

secularism, rise in, 141

security. *See* safety

self-confidence, derived from camp, 45. *See also* interpersonal skills self-contained environment. *See* total environment

self-esteem derived from camp, 45. *See also* interpersonal skills

separation between camp and home. *See* isolated setting

September 11, 2001: impact of on camp culture, 148; and security concerns, 29

service leader and level of engagement, 79

services: and influence of youth culture, 82; similarity to congregation back home, 82.

sessions, length of, 30

Shabbat: effect of Israel experience on observation of, 12; and engagement of campers, 82; importance to staff, 106t; inclusion in site visit, 43; and involvement of Jewish educators, 103; observance of at camp, 27, 37–38, 44, 48, 51, 77, 87–90, 133–34, 143; rituals and customs of, 84, 88, 156n; and staff observance of, 89–90; study program, 64. *See also Havdalah* service; *Kabbalat Shabbat*

Shabbat zemirot (songs celebrating the Sabbath), 84

shacharit (morning prayers): level of engagement in, 53, 80; and role models, 71. *See also t'fillot* (daily prayers)

shaliach. See educators, Jewish; Israeli staff; *shlichim,* Israeli

Sherif, Carolyn and Muzafer, 1, 143

shiurim (lessons), 56, 137

shlichim, Israeli (emissaries), 35. *See also* Israeli staff; Summer *Shlichim* Program

shofar (ram's horn) used for experiential learning, 66, 103

shomrim (guardians of the earth), 52

shortcomings of camp programs, 46, 145

simplicity of camp, 141–42

singing: and integration of Jewish education, 60, 130, 144, 152; and role at camp,

84–85; role in celebration of *Shabbat,* 84, 88–89

site visits, 43–44

size of camp. *See* census of Jewish camps

skullcaps, 52–53

Smith, Rabbi Allan, 39

"social capital," 6

social identity. *See* identity formation

social influence, 13–14

social learning at camp, 14–16, 140

social learning theory, 14

social organization, development of by group, 1

socialization: and camper-camper relations, 15; and camper-staff relations, 3, 15, 32, 140, 153; definition of, 4; and identity formation, 4, 13; and Jewish children, 5, 15, 56; processes, 13–14, 69; role of community in, 5–7

socializing agent, Jewish: camp as a, 3–4, 10–11, 16–18, 21, 24, 41, 43, 55, 140, 145, 151, 153; effectiveness of camp as a, 12–13, 152; limitations of, 12–13; role of Hebrew as, 93–94; and staff role, 119–20, 132, 138. *See also* education, informal Jewish

socializing agents: loss of traditional, 8; need for variety of, 12–13, 17; parents as, 7–8; schools as, 8–10; voluntary nature of, 12

society pages, and announcement of departure to camp, 28

song. *See* singing

song leaders, 79, 80, 84, 85

specialists, 101–3

spirituality, 92, 98, 106t

sponsorship/ownership, 23–24

staff: age of, 124; challenge of hiring, 121; and friendship at camp, 107, 109t, 112t; Jewish educators and rabbis on, 26; knowledge of Judaism, 61–62, 104–5, 119–20, 148; as learners, 15–16, 33, 62, staff (continued)

98, 119, 151; newly hired, 121t; numbers of, 23, 33, 34t, 35; professionalism of, 102, 142; recharging at camp, 33, 102; returning staff, 121t; as role models, 14–15, 71–72, 80–81, 87, 124; and socio-demographic trends, 120. *See also* counselors, bunk

staff-camper relations. *See* socialization

staff from Israel. *See* Israeli staff

staff mentors, 137–38

staff orientation. *See* staff training

staff recruitment, 120, 123, 124

staff shortages, 120, 123–25

staff training, 135–38

standards: and American Camping Association (ACA), 51–53, 131, 153; versus Jewish programming, 51–53

structure. *See* organizational structure

study, description of techniques used, 18

"sukkat shalom" (shelter of peace), 89

Summer *Shlichim* Program, 126–27, 149, 156n

"super campers." *See* counselors-in-training (CITs)

supervisory structure. *See* organizational structure

supportive learning community: and encouragement of risk-taking, 144; and informal education, 66

Surprise Lake, 24

survey of camps. *See* census of Jewish camps

survey of staff, 98–100

symbolism in the environment, 91–92, 143

SYNAGOGUE 2000, 7

synagogues: importance of attendance, 106t; role in creating community, 7

T

tallit (prayer shawl), and use in *Shabbat*, 89

Tamarack Camps, 24

teachable moments, 69–70

teamwork. *See* interpersonal skills; socialization

telephone access at camp, 47, 148

terrorism, concerns about, 29

teva (nature) program: example of, 52; and failure to create opportunity, 74; and symbolism, 91

t'fillot (daily prayers): experimentation with, 10, 143; and level of *kavanah*, 79–80; location of, 92, 93; participation in, 44; and presence of Torah, 81–82; and range of practices at camps, 78–83; repetition of, 78; and role of counselors, 71, 80–81; and service leader, 79; and similarity to home congregation, 82–84. *See also* *shacharit* (morning prayers)

Tikkun olam, 60, 156n

Tishah B'Av, 48, 90–91, 156n

Torah: and engagement of campers, 80; learning of, 79; presence of during *t'fillot*, 81–82; reading of, 156n

total environment: and continuous interaction, 3; and difficulty of counselor job, 122; and success of camp, 46, 48, 69

tradition, strength of, 78, 143. *See also* rituals and customs at camp

travel distance to camp, 29, 46

treif (non-kosher food), 86

trips to Israel. *See* Israel experience

tsofim (scouts), 125, 127

tuition. *See* cost of camp

turnover rate of staff. *See* return rate

types of Jewish camps: and explicit versus implicit educational component, 23; by sponsorship/ownership, 23–28. *See also* *specific types*

U

ultra-Orthodox camps and inclusion in study, 23

unchanging nature of camp, 145–48

under-staffing. *See* staff shortages

Union of American Hebrew Congregations (UAHC), 9, 26, 39, 67, 85, 102

V

values. *See* beliefs

voluntary nature of informal education. *See* education, informal Jewish

voluntary nature of socializing agents. *See* socializing agents

W

welfare, social. *See* Jewish Agency for Israel (JAFI)

worship service. See *t'fillot* (daily prayers)

Y

yeshiva camps, 23, 32

yiddishkeit (Jewishness), 57. *See also* Judaism, engagement in

Yom Yisrael (Israel Day), 40, 67, 129

youth groups, 10, 17, 105

Z

Zeldin, Michael 10, 63

Zionist camps: example of curriculum, 68; examples of goals, 56–57; history of, 25; and Israeli flag as informal education, 144–45; and Israeli staff, 130; and number of Jewish campers, 32; and size of camp, 25; and use of *tsofim*, 127. *See also* movement camps